CROCK·POT®
COOKING

CROCK·POT®
COOKING

ILLUSTRATIONS BY PAT STEWART

GOLDEN PRESS • NEW YORK
WESTERN PUBLISHING COMPANY, INC.
RACINE, WISCONSIN

The Rival Crock-Pot has earned the Good Housekeeping Seal

All the recipes in this cookbook have been reviewed
by the editors of the Good Housekeeping Institute.

Produced in the United States of America.

Library of Congress Catalog Card Number: 75-15197

This book is dedicated to the Crock-Pot cook—

In a very special way. And with our thanks. For had it not been for your interest and that of thousands of other Crock-Pot cooks, we might never have realized that the Crock-Pot deserved an all-new cookbook of recipes—a book to complement the basic recipes and how-to techniques that came with your slow cooker.

Interestingly enough, when Rival developed the Crock-Pot, we believed its major attraction would be the kitchen-free flexibility it would give you. Although we did mention economy at the time, we never dreamed that the present and forecasted shortages and prices would put the Crock-Pot's money-saving abilities so much in the forefront.

Of course, the Crock-Pot's real blessing is that all this economy does not mean dull, monotonous or fork-bending fare. And that's the reason for this book. After many years of testing and tasting, I can guarantee that there are plenty of ideas here to keep your Crock-Pot out and busy. We've included the kinds of recipes you've specifically asked for: a wide variety of meats and main dishes, some interesting party appetizers, special treatments for game, recipes sized just for two and—by popular demand—a special section of diet-wise recipes, complete with calorie counts.

Notice, too, that there is a volume measure following the yield for each and every recipe. Using that measure as a guide, and considering the size of the Crock-Pot you own, you can determine whether to use the recipe as is . . . or whether you can double it. Remember, the ingredients of any recipe must fill at least one and one-half inches of your Crock-Pot.

All of the recipes in this book were developed in the 3½-quart Crock-Pot (except, of course, for the special 6-quart recipes in the "Crock-Pot Specialties" chapter). Timed and tested for use in the Rival Crock-Pot, they may not be satisfactory if prepared in a slow cooker with different characteristics.

Away all day? Flip through the pages for this symbol: ⧖ Every recipe wearing this badge can cook for 9 hours . . . and sometimes longer. What more could a busy cook ask for?

So if you like cooking in a Crock-Pot, you'll love *Crock-Pot Cooking*.

Barbara Brooks

Director of Home Economics
Rival Manufacturing Company

Contents

BEEF, PORK AND LAMB

If for nothing else, your Crock-Pot more than earns its keep
by keeping your meat budget from going completely berserk.
It's ideal for coddling those less expensive cuts of
beef, pork and lamb. It simply takes its time . . .
while you take yours elsewhere.
And this means you can economize anytime,
rather than waiting for a stay-at-home day.
On the following pages, you'll find a repertoire
of main-course meats for every taste and every occasion,
for the family and for company, too.
Whether you choose a roast or ragout, a meat loaf or casserole,
let your Crock-Pot do the cooking for you.

Italian Roast Beef

4-lb. beef rump roast	**1 large stalk celery**
2 onions	**2 oz. salt pork or bacon**
2 cloves garlic	**Flour**

Trim all excess fat from roast. Mince 1 onion, the garlic, celery, and salt pork. Lightly flour roast; rub with minced mixture. Slice remaining onion; place in Crock-Pot. Place roast on onion. Cover and cook on Low setting for 10 to 12 hours.

6 to 8 servings (about 3½ quarts).

Sauerbraten

4-lb. beef rump roast	**3 to 4 whole cloves**
1 cup dry rosé wine	**1 tablespoon salt**
¼ cup cider vinegar	**½ teaspoon pepper**
3 large onions, sliced	**3 tablespoons flour**
2 stalks celery, sliced	**3 tablespoons water**
1 clove garlic	**1 cup crushed gingersnap**
2 whole allspice	**cookies**

Trim roast of all excess fat. In large bowl, combine all ingredients except roast, flour, water and gingersnaps; stir well. Place roast in marinade with fat side down; refrigerate overnight.

Pour vegetable marinade into Crock-Pot. Place marinated roast in Crock-Pot with fat side up. Cover and cook on Low setting for 10 to 12 hours.

Thirty minutes before serving, remove roast and turn to High setting. Make a smooth paste of flour and water; stir into Crock-Pot with gingersnaps. Cook and stir until thickened. Slice roast and return to gravy for serving.

6 to 8 servings (about 3½ quarts).

TO BROWN OR NOT TO BROWN?

You will note that some meats are browned before being used in the Crock-Pot. In Crock-Pot cooking, the purpose of such browning is to eliminate fats (too much fat can cause over-cooking). If the meat is well trimmed and not highly marbled, it need not be browned; it should, however, be wiped thoroughly to absorb all excess juices and any package residue.

America's Favorite Pot Roast

3½- to 4-lb. beef arm or boneless pot roast	2 small onions, sliced
¼ cup flour	1 stalk celery, cut into 2-inch pieces
2 teaspoons salt	1 jar (2 oz.) mushrooms,
⅛ teaspoon pepper	drained, or ¼ cup
3 carrots, pared, sliced	mushroom gravy
lengthwise and cut	3 tablespoons flour
into 2-inch pieces	¼ cup water
3 potatoes, peeled and	
quartered	

Trim all excess fat from roast; brown and drain if using chuck or another highly marbled cut. Combine ¼ cup flour, the salt and pepper. Coat meat with the flour mixture. Place all vegetables except mushrooms in Crock-Pot and top with roast (cut roast in half, if necessary, to fit easily). Spread mushrooms evenly over top of roast. Cover and cook on Low setting for 10 to 12 hours.

If desired, turn to High setting during last hour to soften vegetables and make a gravy. To thicken gravy, make a smooth paste of the 3 tablespoons flour and the water and stir into Crock-Pot. Season to taste before serving.

4 to 6 servings (about 3½ quarts).

Beef Roast with Dried Fruit

2 onions, sliced
3- to 4-lb. beef arm or
  boneless pot roast,
  2 inches thick
1 package (11 oz.) mixed
  dried fruit
¾ cup beer
1 cup water
1 clove garlic, minced

¼ cup brown sugar
  (packed)
1 teaspoon dried parsley
  flakes
1 bay leaf
¼ teaspoon cinnamon
2½ teaspoons salt
¼ teaspoon pepper
Spiced apple rings

Place sliced onions in bottom of Crock-Pot and place roast on top (cut in half, if necessary, to fit easily). Cover with dried fruit. Mix remaining ingredients except apple rings and pour over roast. Cover and cook on Low setting for 10 to 12 hours.

Serve garnished with spiced apple rings.

4 to 6 servings (about 3½ quarts).

Beef Diablo

3- to 4-lb. beef arm or
  boneless pot roast
2 to 3 potatoes, peeled and
  sliced
1 onion, sliced
2 tablespoons flour
1 tablespoon prepared
  mustard

1 tablespoon chili sauce
1 tablespoon Worcester-
  shire sauce
1 teaspoon vinegar
1 teaspoon sugar

Trim all excess fat from roast. Place potatoes and onion in bottom of Crock-Pot.

Make a smooth paste of flour, mustard, chili sauce, Worcestershire sauce, vinegar and sugar. Spread over top of roast (cut roast in half, if necessary, to fit easily). Place roast in Crock-Pot on top of potatoes and onions. Cover and cook on Low setting for 10 to 12 hours (on High setting for 5 to 6 hours).

4 to 6 servings (about 3 quarts).

Bavarian Pot Roast

3- to 4-lb. beef arm pot roast	4 medium apples, cored and quartered
1 teaspoon vegetable oil	1 small onion, sliced
1½ teaspoons salt	½ cup apple juice or water
⅛ teaspoon pepper	
½ teaspoon ground ginger	3 to 4 tablespoons flour
3 whole cloves	3 to 4 tablespoons water

Wipe roast well and trim off all excess fat. Lightly rub top of meat with oil. Dust with salt, pepper and ginger. Insert cloves in roast. Place apples and onions in Crock-Pot and top with roast (cut roast in half, if necessary, to fit easily). Pour in apple juice. Cover and cook on Low setting for 10 to 12 hours.

Remove roast and apples to warm platter. Turn Crock-Pot to High setting. Make a smooth paste of the flour and water; stir into Crock-Pot. Cover and cook until thickened.

6 to 8 servings (about 3½ quarts).

A WAY WITH VEGETABLES
Because vegetables tend to cook slowly, cut them into ⅛- to ¼-inch slices and place them near the bottom of the Crock-Pot.

Glazed Corned Beef

1 bay leaf
1 medium onion, sliced
2 to 3 strips of fresh
   orange peel (about
   2 inches each)
3 whole cloves

1½ cups water
3- to 4-lb. corned beef
   (preferably round or
   rump cut)
Glaze (below)

Combine all ingredients except corned beef and Glaze in Crock-Pot. Add corned beef with fat side up. Cover and cook on Low setting for 10 to 12 hours or until fork tender (on High setting for 5 to 6 hours).

Remove meat from broth. Score top of corned beef in diamond shapes. Insert additional cloves to decorate.

About 30 minutes before serving, place corned beef on heatproof platter. Prepare Glaze and spoon over corned beef. Bake in 375° oven for 20 to 30 minutes, basting occasionally with Glaze.

8 to 10 servings (about 3½ quarts).

GLAZE

3 tablespoons frozen
   orange juice concen-
   trate, thawed

3 tablespoons honey
1 tablespoon Dijon mustard

Mix together until smooth and blended.

Simple Brisket

4- to 5-lb. fresh beef brisket
1 envelope (1½ oz.) dry
   onion soup mix

1 can (4 oz.) mushrooms,
   undrained

Trim all excess fat from brisket. Combine onion soup mix with mushrooms and their liquid. Place brisket in Crock-Pot with fat side up, cutting to fit if necessary. Spread onion soup mixture over top of brisket, moistening well. Cover and cook on Low setting for 10 to 14 hours.

Remove brisket and cut across the grain into thin slices. Serve with meat juices poured over top of slices.

8 to 10 servings (about 3½ quarts).

Marinated Barbecue Brisket

4- to 5-lb. fresh beef brisket
2 teaspoons unseasoned
   meat tenderizer
½ teaspoon celery salt
½ teaspoon seasoned salt

½ teaspoon garlic salt
¼ cup liquid smoke
¼ cup Worcestershire
   sauce
1½ cups barbecue sauce

Place brisket on large piece of heavy-duty aluminum foil. Sprinkle tenderizer and seasonings on both sides of meat. Pour liquid smoke and Worcestershire sauce over top. Cover and marinate in refrigerator 6 to 10 hours or overnight.

Place foil-wrapped brisket in Crock-Pot (cut brisket in half, if necessary, to fit easily). Cover and cook on Low setting for 10 to 12 hours.

Chill brisket, then cut across the grain into thin slices. Before serving, reheat in your favorite barbecue sauce.

8 to 10 servings (about 3½ quarts).

Favorite Brisket

4-lb. fresh beef brisket
2 teaspoons salt
2 teaspoons dry mustard
2 teaspoons paprika

⅛ teaspoon pepper
½ to 1 teaspoon garlic
  powder

Trim all excess fat from brisket. Combine seasonings until well blended; rub into brisket. Place meat in Crock-Pot with fat side up, cutting to fit if necessary. Cover and cook on Low setting for 10 to 12 hours.

Remove brisket from liquid and cut across the grain into thin slices. Serve au jus.

6 to 8 servings (about 3 quarts).

Boiled Beef with Vegetables

2-lb. fresh beef brisket or
  stewing beef
1 marrow bone
2 carrots, pared, sliced
  lengthwise and
  quartered
2 turnips, peeled and cut
  into 1-inch cubes

6 small white onions
¼ teaspoon leaf thyme
1 bay leaf
2 whole cloves
2 cups beef broth or water
Salt
1 medium cabbage, cut
  into wedges

Place all ingredients except cabbage in Crock-Pot; stir well. Cover and cook on Low setting for 10 to 12 hours.

Before serving, remove 1 cup of broth from Crock-Pot. Pour into skillet; add cabbage wedges and simmer until tender. Cut meat across the grain and serve on a hot platter with vegetables. Serve with broth.

6 to 8 servings (about 3½ quarts).

Cholent

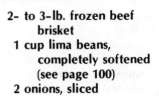

2- to 3-lb. frozen beef brisket	1 cup water
1 cup lima beans, completely softened (see page 100)	2 teaspoons garlic salt
2 onions, sliced	¼ teaspoon coarsely ground pepper
	¼ teaspoon paprika

Trim all excess fat from brisket. Combine softened lima beans, onions and water in Crock-Pot; mix well. Add brisket and seasonings. Cover and cook on Low setting for 16 to 24 hours. Serve sliced meat over limas and onions with the natural juices over all.

4 to 6 servings (about 3 quarts).

Flank Steak Teriyaki

2-lb. beef flank steak	2 tablespoons brown sugar
6 slices canned juice-pack pineapple (reserve ½ cup juice)	1 teaspoon Worcestershire sauce
2 tablespoons soy sauce	2 chicken bouillon cubes
½ teaspoon ground ginger	1½ cups boiling water
1 tablespoon dry sherry	1 cup raw long-grain converted rice

Roll flank steak, tie and cut into 6 individual steaks. In shallow bowl, stir together pineapple juice, soy sauce, ginger, sherry, sugar and Worcestershire sauce. Marinate steaks about 1 hour in soy mixture at room temperature. Dissolve bouillon cubes in boiling water; combine with rice and ½ cup of soy mixture in Crock-Pot. Top each steak with a pineapple ring, then place in Crock-Pot. Cover and cook on Low setting for 8 to 10 hours (on High setting for 3 to 4 hours).

6 servings (about 2½ quarts).

Smothered Flank Steak

2½-lb. beef flank or round
   steak
Salt and pepper
1 tablespoon Worcester-
   shire sauce
1 tablespoon vegetable oil
Paprika

2 medium onions, thinly
   sliced
½ lb. mushrooms, sliced,
   or 2 cans (4 oz. each)
   sliced mushrooms,
   drained
Chopped parsley

With sharp knife, score meat about 1/8 inch deep in diamond pattern on top side. Season with salt and pepper. Rub in Worcestershire sauce and oil. Sprinkle top with paprika. Place sliced onions and mushrooms in Crock-Pot. Roll flank steak, if necessary to fit easily, and place on top of onions. Cover and cook on Low setting for 8 to 10 hours.

Remove steak to warm carving platter and cut across the grain in thin diagonal slices. Serve with onions and mushrooms, pouring unthickened gravy over all. Sprinkle with parsley.

6 servings (about 2½ quarts).

Flemish Carbonnades

2-lb. round steak, 1 inch
   thick
¼ cup flour
1 teaspoon sugar
⅛ teaspoon pepper

6 to 8 small new potatoes,
   peeled
1 envelope (1½ oz.) dry
   onion soup mix
¾ cup beer

Trim round steak and cut into serving portions. Combine flour, sugar and pepper; toss with steak to coat thoroughly. Place potatoes in Crock-Pot and cover with steak pieces. Thoroughly combine onion soup mix and beer. Pour over steak, moistening well. Cover and cook on Low setting for 8 to 12 hours. Thicken gravy before serving, if desired.

4 to 6 servings (about 3 quarts).

Savory Pepper Steak

1½- to 2-lb. beef round steak, about ½ inch thick
¼ cup flour
½ teaspoon salt
⅛ teaspoon pepper
1 medium onion, chopped
1 small clove garlic, minced
2 large green peppers, seeded and cut into ½-inch strips

1 can (16 oz.) whole tomatoes
1 tablespoon beef flavor base (paste or granules)
1 tablespoon soy sauce
2 teaspoons Worcestershire sauce
Fluffy rice

Cut steak into strips. Combine ¼ cup flour, the salt and pepper; toss with steak strips to coat thoroughly. Add to Crock-Pot with onion, garlic and half of green pepper strips; stir.

Combine tomatoes with beef base, soy sauce and Worcestershire sauce. Pour into Crock-Pot, moistening meat well. Cover and cook on Low setting for 8 to 10 hours.

One hour before serving, turn to High setting and stir in remaining green pepper strips. If thickened gravy is desired, make a smooth paste of 3 tablespoons flour and 3 tablespoons water; stir into Crock-Pot. Cover and cook until thickened. Serve gravy with Pepper Steak over hot fluffy rice.

4 servings (about 2 quarts).

Beef Roulades

1½-lb. beef round steak, ½ inch thick	¾ cup diced onion
4 slices bacon	½ cup diced green pepper
¾ cup diced celery	1 can (10 oz.) beef gravy

Cut steak into four serving pieces. Place bacon slice on each piece of meat. Mix celery, onion and green pepper; place about ½ cup mixture on each piece of meat. Roll up meat; secure ends with wooden picks.

Wipe beef rolls with paper towels. Place in Crock-Pot. Pour gravy evenly over steaks to thoroughly moisten. Cover Crock-Pot and cook on Low setting for 8 to 10 hours. Skim off fat before serving.

4 servings (about 2½ quarts).

Beef Stroganoff

3-lb. beef round steak, ½ inch thick	1 can (10½ oz.) condensed beef broth
½ cup flour	¼ cup dry white wine (optional)
2 teaspoons salt	1½ cups sour cream
⅛ teaspoon pepper	¼ cup flour
½ teaspoon dry mustard	Hot buttered noodles or fluffy rice
2 medium onions, thinly sliced and separated into rings	3 tablespoons fresh minced parsley
2 cans (4 oz. each) sliced mushrooms, drained, or ½ lb. mushrooms, sliced	

Trim all excess fat from steak and cut meat into 3-inch strips about ½ inch wide. Combine ½ cup flour, the salt, pepper and dry mustard; toss with steak strips to coat thoroughly. Place coated steak strips in Crock-Pot; stir in onion rings and mushrooms. Add beef broth and wine; stir well. Cover and cook on Low setting for 8 to 10 hours.

Before serving, combine sour cream with ¼ cup flour; stir into Crock-Pot. Serve Stroganoff over hot buttered noodles; garnish with minced parsley.

8 servings (about 3 quarts).

Braciole

2½-lb. round steak, ¼ to ½ inch thick	1 large onion, finely chopped
½ lb. bulk Italian sausage	1 teaspoon salt
1 tablespoon dried parsley flakes	1 can (16 oz.) Italian-style tomatoes
½ teaspoon leaf oregano	1 can (6 oz.) tomato paste
2 small cloves garlic, minced	1 teaspoon salt
	1 teaspoon leaf oregano

Trim all excess fat from round steak. Cut into 8 evenly shaped pieces. Pound steak pieces between waxed paper until very thin and easy to roll. In skillet, lightly brown sausage. Drain well and combine with parsley, ½ teaspoon oregano, the garlic, onion and salt; mix well. Spread each steak with 2 to 3 tablespoons of sausage mixture. Roll up jelly-roll fashion and tie.

Stack steak rolls in Crock-Pot. Combine tomatoes, tomato paste, salt and 1 teaspoon oregano; pour over rolls. Cover and cook on Low setting for 8 to 10 hours.

Serve steak rolls with sauce.

8 servings (about 3 quarts).

Swiss Steak

2-lb. beef round steak, about 1 inch thick	**¼ cup chopped onion**
¼ cup flour	**½ teaspoon Worcestershire sauce**
1 teaspoon salt	**1 can (16 oz.) whole tomatoes**
1 stalk celery, chopped	**½ cup grated process American cheese**
2 carrots, pared and chopped	

Cut steak into 4 serving pieces. Dredge in flour mixed with salt; place in Crock-Pot. Add chopped vegetables and Worcestershire sauce. Pour tomatoes over meat and vegetables. Cover and cook on Low setting for 8 to 10 hours.

Just before serving, sprinkle with grated cheese.

4 servings (about 2 quarts). Recipe may be doubled for 5-quart Crock-Pot. Cook the maximum time.

Marinated Beef

2-lb. beef round steak, very thinly sliced	**2 tablespoons flour**
1 cup white wine	**2 tablespoons butter, melted**
¼ teaspoon leaf thyme	**Salt and pepper**
1 bay leaf	**2 to 3 tablespoons chopped parsley**
4 peppercorns	
3 medium onions, sliced	

Place steak slices in bowl. Mix together white wine, thyme, bay leaf and peppercorns and pour over steak. Cover and refrigerate until morning.

Place alternate layers of sliced onion and meat in Crock-Pot. Pour in marinade. Cover and cook on Low setting for 8 to 10 hours.

One hour before serving, mix flour and butter; add to Crock-Pot. Taste for seasoning. Continue to cook until thickened. Serve sprinkled with chopped parsley.

4 servings (about 2½ quarts).

English Beef Pot Pie

2 lb. beef round steak, cut into 1-inch cubes
3 tablespoons flour
1 teaspoon salt
⅛ teaspoon pepper
2 medium carrots, pared and sliced
3 medium potatoes, peeled and sliced
1 large onion, thinly sliced
1 can (16 oz.) whole tomatoes
Biscuit Topping (below)

Place steak cubes in Crock-Pot. Combine flour, salt and pepper; toss with steak to coat thoroughly. Stir in remaining ingredients except Biscuit Topping and mix thoroughly. Cover and cook on Low setting for 8 to 10 hours.

One hour before serving, remove meat and vegetables from Crock-Pot and pour into shallow 2½-quart baking dish. Preheat oven to 425°. Cover meat mixture with Biscuit Topping. Bake for 20 to 25 minutes.

4 servings (about 2½ quarts).

BISCUIT TOPPING

2 cups flour
1 teaspoon salt
3 teaspoons baking powder
¼ cup shortening
¾ cup milk

Mix dry ingredients. Cut in shortening until mixture resembles coarse cornmeal. Add milk all at one time; stir well. Pat out on floured board; roll out to cover baking dish.

Steak and Kidney Pie

1½ lb. beef kidneys
1½ lb. beef round steak or
    chuck, well trimmed
    and cut into 1½-inch
    cubes
1 onion, thinly sliced

1 cup beef broth
1 teaspoon salt
½ teaspoon pepper
    Prepared pie crust or
    biscuit topping

Cook kidney in salted water for 8 minutes; drain and pat dry. Trim off excess fat and cut kidney into cubes. Combine kidney, steak and onion in Crock-Pot. Add beef broth, salt and pepper. Cover and cook on Low setting for 8 to 10 hours (on High setting for 3 to 4 hours).

Remove contents of Crock-Pot to baking dish; cover with pie crust. Bake in preheated 400° oven for 15 to 20 minutes.

4 servings (about 2 quarts).

NOTE: This freezes beautifully; add crust just before baking.

Crock-Pot Curry

3 lb. beef round steak or
    lean stewing beef, cut
    into 1½-inch cubes
½ cup flour
1 tablespoon curry powder
2 cloves garlic, minced
1 cup raisins
2 apples, peeled, cored and
    sliced

1 cup diced onion
2 teaspoons salt
½ teaspoon pepper
1 can (14 oz.) beef broth
2 apples (unpeeled), cored
    and finely chopped
    Fluffy rice

Wipe beef well. Mix flour and curry powder. Coat meat cubes with flour mixture. Place meat in Crock-Pot. Add garlic, raisins, sliced apples, onion, salt and pepper. Pour in broth and stir to blend. Cover and cook on Low setting for 8 to 10 hours or until meat is tender.

Before serving, stir in additional curry powder to taste (up to 1 tablespoon) and chopped apples. Serve over hot rice.

6 to 8 servings (about 2½ quarts).

NOTE: Three pounds cubed lean lamb may be substituted for the beef.

Beef Tips

½ cup flour
1 teaspoon salt
⅛ teaspoon pepper
4 lb. beef or sirloin tips
½ cup chopped shallots or green onions
2 cans (4 oz. each) sliced mushrooms, drained, or ½ lb. mushrooms, sliced

1 can (10½ oz.) condensed beef broth
1 teaspoon Worcestershire sauce
2 teaspoons tomato paste or ketchup
¼ cup dry red wine or water
3 tablespoons flour
Buttered noodles

Combine ½ cup flour with the salt and pepper and toss with beef cubes to coat thoroughly. Place in Crock-Pot. Add shallots and mushrooms. Combine beef broth, Worcestershire sauce and tomato paste. Pour over beef and vegetables; stir well. Cover and cook on Low setting for 8 to 12 hours.

One hour before serving, turn to High setting. Make a smooth paste of red wine and 3 tablespoons flour; stir into Crock-Pot, mixing well. Cover and cook until thickened. Serve over hot buttered noodles.

8 to 10 servings (about 3 quarts).

Crock-Pot Stew

3 to 4 lb. beef round or
chuck steak, 1½ inches
thick, cut into 1½-inch
cubes
⅓ cup flour
1 teaspoon salt
½ teaspoon cracked pepper
2 to 3 carrots, pared, split
lengthwise and cut in
half
2 large stalks celery, cut
into 1-inch pieces
6 small white onions
6 to 8 small new potatoes,
peeled
1 can (4 oz.) sliced mushrooms, drained

1 package (10 oz.) frozen
peas, corn, green beans
or lima beans, partially
thawed
1 can (10½ oz.) condensed
beef broth
½ cup dry red wine or
water
2 teaspoons brown sugar
2 teaspoons Kitchen
Bouquet
1 can (14½ oz.) tomato
wedges or slices,
drained (optional)
¼ cup flour
¼ cup water

If beef is extra lean, thoroughly wipe cubed beef on absorbent towels to dry. If meat contains fat, quickly brown in
large skillet to sear and remove fat; drain well.

Place beef cubes in Crock-Pot. Combine ⅓ cup flour with
the salt and pepper; toss with beef to coat thoroughly. Add
all vegetables except tomato wedges to Crock-Pot and mix
well. Combine beef broth, wine, sugar and Kitchen Bouquet.
Pour over meat and vegetables; stir carefully. Add drained
tomatoes and stir well. Cover and cook on Low setting for
10 to 14 hours (on High setting for 4 to 5½ hours).

One hour before serving, turn to High setting. Make a
smooth paste of ¼ cup flour and the water; stir into Crock-
Pot. Cover and cook until thickened.

8 to 10 servings (about 3½ quarts).

NOTE: For better color, add half of the frozen vegetables at
beginning; add remaining half during last hour.

Hearty Beef Ragout

3 lb. boneless beef chuck,
    cut into 1-inch pieces
⅓ cup flour
2 teaspoons salt
¼ teaspoon pepper
1 package (8 oz.) precooked
    sausage links, cut into
    1-inch pieces
2 cups chopped leeks
3 to 4 stalks celery, cut up
3 potatoes, peeled and
    cubed

1 can (16 oz.) whole
    tomatoes
1 teaspoon leaf oregano
2 cloves garlic, minced
½ cup beef broth
1 teaspoon Kitchen
    Bouquet
2 tablespoons flour
3 tablespoons water

Wipe beef well. Combine ⅓ cup flour with salt and pepper. Toss beef cubes with flour mixture to coat thoroughly; place in Crock-Pot. Add remaining ingredients except 2 tablespoons flour and the water in order listed; stir well. Cover and cook on Low setting for 8 to 12 hours.

One hour before serving, turn to High setting. Make a smooth paste of 2 tablespoons flour and the water; stir into Crock-Pot, mixing well. Cover and cook until thickened.

8 servings (about 3 quarts).

HERBS AND SPICES: THE FLAVOR SAVORS
It's best to use whole herbs and spices rather than the crushed or ground forms. The flavor of crushed or ground herbs and spices tends to dissipate during the extended cooking times called for in the Crock-Pot. The leaf form, on the other hand, takes a much longer time to release its flavor; hence, it will be nearer its peak at serving time. Always taste before serving, and adjust the seasonings if necessary.

Nabil's Grecian Beef Stew

2 lb. lean stewing beef,
cut into 1½-inch
cubes
2 onions, sliced
2 cloves garlic, chopped
2 tablespoons vegetable
oil
1 eggplant (unpeeled),
cubed
1 cup beef broth
2½ teaspoons cinnamon

2 teaspoons salt
Pepper
1 can (16 oz.) garbanzos,
drained
1 can (16 oz.) tomato
wedges, drained
1 tablespoon Kitchen
Bouquet
Fluffy rice
Minced parsley

In large skillet, brown beef, onions and garlic in oil; drain. Place in Crock-Pot.

Parboil eggplant in 2 cups boiling salted water for 2 minutes; drain. Add to beef mixture; stir well. Combine beef broth with cinnamon, salt and pepper and pour into Crock-Pot; stir well. Cover and cook on Low setting for 10 to 12 hours.

One hour before serving, stir in garbanzos, tomato wedges and Kitchen Bouquet.

4 to 6 servings (about 3 quarts).

Bachelor's Stew

2 lb. beef chuck, cut into
   1- to 2-inch cubes
⅓ cup dry bread crumbs
1 teaspoon salt
⅛ teaspoon pepper
1 large onion, cut into
   eighths
3 carrots, pared, split
   lengthwise and cut
   into 4-inch strips
4 celery stalks, cut into
   1-inch pieces

1 teaspoon leaf basil
⅓ cup quick-cooking
   tapioca
1 can (4 oz.) sliced mushrooms, undrained
1 teaspoon Kitchen
   Bouquet
2 cans (10¾ oz. each)
   condensed tomato soup
1 cup beef broth or water

Wipe beef cubes well. Combine bread crumbs with salt and
pepper and toss with beef. Place coated beef cubes in Crock-
Pot and add remaining ingredients; stir well. Cover and cook
on Low setting for 10 to 12 hours (on High setting for 3 to 5
hours).

6 servings (about 3 quarts).

Good 'n Easy Stew

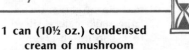

3 lb. lean stewing beef,
   cut into 1½-inch cubes
1 envelope (1½ oz.) dry
   onion soup mix
½ cup sauterne wine or
   beef broth

1 can (10½ oz.) condensed
   cream of mushroom
   soup or cream of
   celery soup
1 can (4 oz.) sliced mushrooms, drained
   (optional)

Combine all ingredients in Crock-Pot. Cover and cook on Low
setting for 10 to 12 hours. If desired, thicken gravy.

8 servings (about 3 quarts).

Hungarian Beef Stew

2 lb. lean stewing beef,
cut into 1½-inch
cubes
1 large onion, finely
chopped
2 medium potatoes,
peeled and cubed
2 carrots, pared and sliced
1 package (10 oz.) frozen
lima beans, thawed

2 cloves garlic, chopped
1 green pepper, seeded
and cut into strips
2 teaspoons dried parsley
flakes
½ cup beef broth
2 teaspoons paprika
1½ teaspoons salt
1 can (16 oz.) whole
tomatoes

Place all ingredients except beef broth, paprika, salt and tomatoes in Crock-Pot. Mix beef broth, paprika, salt and tomatoes; pour over top and stir to blend. Cover and cook on
Low setting for 10 to 12 hours.

4 to 6 servings (about 2½ quarts).

Stairwell Stew

2 lb. lean stewing beef,
cut into 1½-inch cubes
1 to 2 cloves garlic, sliced
2 large stalks celery, sliced
¼ to ½ cup pitted green
olives, drained
1 can (4 oz.) sliced mushrooms, drained

1 can (16 oz.) whole
tomatoes
2 tablespoons flour
2 tablespoons water
Grated mozzarella cheese
(optional)

Trim and wipe stew meat thoroughly. Combine all ingredients except flour, water and mozzarella cheese in Crock-Pot.
Cover and cook on Low setting for 10 to 12 hours (on High setting for 3 to 4 hours).

One hour before serving, turn to High setting. Make a smooth paste of flour and water; stir into Crock-Pot. Cover and cook until thickened. Sprinkle mozzarella cheese generously over top.

4 to 6 servings (about 2½ quarts).

NOTE: A 3-lb. cut-up chicken or round steak may be substituted for the stewing beef.

Braised Oxtails

3 to 4 lb. oxtails, cut into pieces	1 bay leaf
2 onions, thinly sliced	2 teaspoons salt
1 carrot, pared and sliced	⅛ teaspoon pepper
3 potatoes, peeled and cubed	1 cup beef broth
1 turnip, peeled and cubed (optional)	3 tablespoons ketchup
½ teaspoon leaf thyme	3 tablespoons flour
	¼ cup water or red wine
	¼ cup chopped parsley

Place oxtails on broiler rack and broil for 15 to 20 minutes to brown and remove fat; drain. Place browned oxtails in Crock-Pot. Add all remaining ingredients except flour, water and parsley; stir well and push vegetables down to be covered and moistened by broth. Cover and cook on Low setting for 10 to 12 hours.

One hour before serving, turn to High setting. Make a smooth paste of flour and water; stir into Crock-Pot. Cover and cook until thickened. Sprinkle with chopped parsley before serving.

6 servings (about 3½ quarts).

Beef Shanks with Gravy

1 medium onion, thinly sliced	Salt
2 carrots, pared and thinly sliced	2 cans (10¾ oz. each) condensed tomato soup
2 stalks celery, sliced	2 lb. cross-cut beef shanks
4 peppercorns	3 tablespoons flour (optional)
2 whole cloves	3 tablespoons water (optional)
2 tablespoons brown sugar	
2 tablespoons vinegar	

Combine all ingredients except beef shanks, flour and water in Crock-Pot; stir well. Add beef shanks, pushing down to coat with tomato mixture. Cover and cook on Low setting for 10 to 12 hours.

Remove meat with slotted spoon. Bone and cut meat into small pieces; return to gravy.

If thickened gravy is desired, make a smooth paste of the flour and water. Turn to High setting and stir in paste. Cover and cook for 1 hour or until gravy is thickened.

6 servings (about 2½ quarts).

Individual Pot Roasts

4 to 5 small cross-cut beef shanks	2 large baking potatoes, peeled and sliced ¼ inch thick
1 envelope (1½ oz.) dry onion soup mix	2 medium carrots, pared and halved lengthwise
2 cans (4 oz. each) sliced mushrooms, drained and liquid reserved	

Wipe beef shanks well. Thoroughly combine onion soup mix and liquid from mushrooms; stir in sliced mushrooms. Spread a small amount of mushroom mixture on top of each beef shank.

Place sliced potatoes and carrots in bottom of Crock-Pot. Place beef shanks on top of vegetables. Pour any remaining mushroom mixture over the top. Cover and cook on Low setting for 10 to 12 hours.

Serve with unthickened gravy poured over top.

4 to 5 servings (about 3½ quarts).

Braised Short Ribs

3 to 4 lb. lean beef short ribs	1 clove garlic, chopped (optional)
½ cup flour	1 cup beer, beef broth or water
1½ teaspoons paprika	2 tablespoons flour (optional)
1½ teaspoons salt	3 tablespoons water (optional)
½ teaspoon dry mustard	
2 medium onions, sliced and separated into rings	

Place short ribs on broiler rack or in skillet and brown to remove fat; drain well. Combine ½ cup flour with the paprika, salt and dry mustard; toss with short ribs. Place remaining ingredients except 2 tablespoons flour and the water in Crock-Pot; stir to mix beef ribs with onion rings (be sure onions are under beef ribs—not on top). Cover and cook on Low setting for 8 to 12 hours.

Remove short ribs to warm serving platter. If thickened gravy is desired, make a smooth paste of flour and water. Turn Crock-Pot to High setting and stir in paste. Cover and cook until gravy is thickened.

6 servings (about 3 quarts).

Beef Hash

2 to 3 cups cut-up cooked beef
2 packages (10 oz. each) frozen hash brown potatoes, thawed

1 onion, finely chopped
¼ cup butter or margarine, melted
1 cup gravy or beef broth
Salt and pepper

Place all ingredients in Crock-Pot. Cover and cook on Low setting for 6 to 8 hours (on High setting for 2 to 3 hours).

4 servings (about 1½ quarts). Double recipe for 5-quart Crock-Pot.

Barbecued Meat Loaf

2 lb. ground chuck or lean ground beef
½ cup uncooked quick or old-fashioned oats
½ cup dry bread crumbs
2 tablespoons non-fat dry milk solids
½ cup water

½ cup bottled smoky barbecue sauce
2 eggs
1 teaspoon salt
¼ teaspoon pepper
1 small onion, chopped
6 potatoes, cut up

In large bowl, mix all ingredients except potatoes. Shape meat mixture into a loaf. Place potatoes in bottom of Crock-Pot. Top potatoes with meat loaf. Cover and cook on Low for 8 to 10 hours.

6 servings (about 3 quarts).

Peppered Meat Loaf

2 lb. ground chuck
½ lb. bulk sausage
1 large onion, finely
    chopped
3 cloves garlic, minced
1 can (8 oz.) tomato sauce
½ cup ketchup
¾ cup crushed saltine
    crackers

2 eggs
2 teaspoons Worcestershire
    sauce
2 teaspoons seasoned salt
¼ teaspoon seasoned
    pepper
1 to 2 potatoes, peeled and
    cut into fingers
Sauce (below)

Combine all ingredients except potatoes and Sauce; mix well and shape into a loaf. Place potatoes in bottom of Crock-Pot. Top potatoes with meat loaf. Pour Sauce over all. Cover and cook on Low setting for 8 to 12 hours.

6 to 8 servings (about 2½ quarts).

SAUCE

1 cup ketchup
⅓ cup brown sugar

1½ teaspoons dry mustard
½ teaspoon nutmeg

Mix ingredients well.

Gourmet Meat Loaf

1 slice bread	8 dried apricots, soaked
¼ cup milk	and chopped
1 egg, beaten	¼ cup chutney
1 medium onion, chopped	Salt and pepper
1½ teaspoons curry powder	1½ lb. ground beef
2 teaspoons lemon juice	2 bay leaves, broken in
¼ cup chopped almonds	several pieces

Soak bread in milk; squeeze dry. Mix egg with milk. Add all ingredients except bay leaves to ground beef; blend well. Shape into a loaf. Insert bay leaves in top of meat loaf. Place in Crock-Pot. Cover and cook on Low setting for 8 to 10 hours. Remove bay leaves before serving.

4 to 6 servings (about 2 quarts).

Norwegian Meatballs in Sauce

1½ lb. extra-lean ground	¼ teaspoon allspice
beef	¼ teaspoon ground ginger
½ lb. extra-lean ground	¼ teaspoon black pepper
pork or veal	¼ teaspoon nutmeg
1 egg	½ teaspoon brown sugar
1 cup mashed potatoes	½ cup flour
½ cup dry bread crumbs	1 cup beef broth
½ cup milk	½ cup heavy cream
2 teaspoons seasoned salt	½ cup chopped parsley
¼ teaspoon ground cloves	

Thoroughly combine all ingredients except flour, beef broth, heavy cream and chopped parsley. Blend well and shape into about twenty-four 1½-inch meatballs. Roll lightly in flour. Place on rack of broiler pan in preheated 400° oven for 20 minutes. Drain and place in Crock-Pot. Pour beef broth over meatballs. Cover and cook on Low setting for 7 to 9 hours (on High setting for 2 to 3 hours).

Before serving, carefully remove meatballs to warm platter. Stir heavy cream into broth in Crock-Pot; mix until smooth. Pour sauce over meatballs, then sprinkle with the chopped parsley.

6 to 8 servings (about 2½ quarts).

Meatballs in Gravy

1 lb. lean ground beef
¼ lb. ground veal
¼ lb. lean ground pork
¼ lb. bulk sausage
1 egg
2 tablespoons dried
   parsley flakes
½ cup grated Parmesan
   cheese
1½ teaspoons salt
¼ teaspoon pepper
1½ cups fresh bread crumbs
Gravy (below)

Mix thoroughly all ingredients except Gravy. Shape into meatballs and brown in skillet or on broiler rack in 400° oven. Prepare Gravy in Crock-Pot. Add meatballs. Cover and cook on Low setting for 7 to 9 hours (on High setting for 3 to 4 hours).

4 to 6 servings (about 2 quarts).

GRAVY

1 can (4 oz.) mushrooms,
   drained
1 can (10¾ oz.) condensed
   cream of mushroom
   soup
1 cup sour cream
⅓ cup flour
½ teaspoon instant coffee
¼ cup dry sherry
1 teaspoon paprika

Combine all ingredients in Crock-Pot; stir thoroughly.

Meatball Stew

1 lb. lean ground beef
1 medium onion, chopped
1 egg
1 cup dry bread crumbs
½ teaspoon salt
¼ teaspoon pepper
2 tablespoons margarine
    or butter
1 can (16 oz.) whole
    tomatoes, undrained,
    chopped
1 cup water
2 tablespoons beef flavor
    base (paste or
    granules)

¼ teaspoon garlic powder
½ teaspoon seasoned salt
2 teaspoons Italian
    seasoning
4 carrots, pared and sliced
3 large potatoes, peeled
    and diced
1 medium onion, sliced
2 tablespoons cornstarch
¼ cup cold water

Combine ground beef with chopped onion, egg, bread crumbs, salt and pepper. Shape mixture into about 24 meatballs, then brown in margarine; drain well.

Stir together tomatoes, water, beef base and seasonings. Place carrots, potatoes and sliced onion in bottom of Crock-Pot; top with meatballs. Pour tomato mixture over all. Cover and cook on Low setting for 8 to 10 hours.

Before serving, remove meatballs with a slotted spoon. Make a smooth paste of the cornstarch and water and stir into vegetables. Cover and cook on High setting for 10 minutes to thicken. Return meatballs to stew and serve.

6 servings (about 3 quarts).

Hamburger Hot Pot

1½ lb. ground chuck or
    lean ground beef
¼ teaspoon garlic powder
2 teaspoons salt
¼ teaspoon pepper
6 medium potatoes,
    peeled and sliced

3 medium onions, sliced
1 can (10¾ oz.) condensed
    golden mushroom soup
½ cup water

In skillet, lightly brown ground beef; drain well. Add garlic powder, salt and pepper; set aside. Place half the potatoes and half the onions in greased Crock-Pot. Add browned beef. Top with remaining potatoes and onions. Combine mushroom soup and water; spread over top, being sure to moisten and cover evenly. Cover and cook on Low setting for 8 to 10 hours (on High setting for 3 to 4 hours).

4 to 6 servings (about 2½ quarts).

Barbecue Burgers

1½ lb. ground chuck
3 potatoes, peeled and
    thinly sliced
½ cup ketchup
1 onion, finely chopped

2 tablespoons sugar
1 tablespoon cider vinegar
1 tablespoon Worcester-
    shire sauce

Shape ground chuck into 6 burgers. Place sliced potatoes in Crock-Pot. Combine remaining ingredients and coat each burger with sauce mixture; arrange over potatoes in Crock-Pot. Cover and cook on Low setting for 8 to 10 hours.

6 servings (about 2½ quarts).

NOTE: If you have the accessory Meat Rack, place over potatoes and arrange burgers on rack.

Stuffed Cabbage

12 large cabbage leaves
1 lb. lean ground beef or lamb
½ cup cooked rice
½ teaspoon salt
⅛ teaspoon pepper
¼ teaspoon leaf thyme
¼ teaspoon nutmeg
¼ teaspoon cinnamon
1 can (6 oz.) tomato paste
¾ cup water

Wash cabbage leaves. Boil 4 cups water. Turn heat off. Soak leaves in water for 5 minutes. Remove, drain and cool.

Combine remaining ingredients except tomato paste and water. Place 2 tablespoons of mixture on each leaf and roll firmly. Stack in Crock-Pot. Combine tomato paste and water and pour over stuffed cabbage. Cover and cook on Low setting for 8 to 10 hours.

6 servings (about 2½ quarts).

Layered Enchilada Casserole

1 can (14½ oz.) whole tomatoes
1 small onion, cut into pieces
1 clove garlic, minced
½ teaspoon ground red pepper
½ teaspoon salt
1 can (6 oz.) tomato paste
1 lb. ground beef, browned
2 cups (8 oz.) shredded Cheddar cheese
9 corn tortillas

To prepare sauce, blend tomatoes and their liquid with onion and garlic in a blender or food processor. Pour into medium-sized saucepan. Add red pepper, salt and tomato paste. Heat to a boil; then simmer for 5 to 10 minutes.

Place 3 tortillas in bottom of Crock-Pot. Layer on tortillas ⅓ of the ground beef, ⅓ of the tomato sauce and ⅓ of the Cheddar cheese. Repeat each layer two more times. Cover and cook on Low 6 to 8 hours.

4 servings

Brunch Casserole

1½ lb. lean ground beef
1 large onion, finely chopped
2 tablespoons olive oil or butter
2 cloves garlic, minced
1 can (4 oz.) sliced mushrooms, drained
2 teaspoons salt
½ teaspoon nutmeg

½ teaspoon leaf oregano
½ package (10 oz.) frozen chopped spinach, thawed and drained
3 tablespoons flour
6 eggs, beaten
¾ cup milk, scalded
½ cup grated sharp Cheddar cheese

In skillet, lightly brown ground beef and onion in olive oil; drain well. Place in well-greased Crock-Pot. Stir in remaining ingredients except eggs, milk and cheese until well blended.

Beat eggs and milk together. Pour over other ingredients; stir well. Dust with additional nutmeg. Cover and cook on Low setting for 7 to 9 hours or until firm.

Just before serving, sprinkle with grated cheese.

6 to 8 servings (about 2½ quarts).

Chuckwagon Beef

1 lb. extra-lean ground
  beef
1 can (16 oz.) whole
  tomatoes
1 green pepper, seeded
  and finely chopped
1 onion, finely chopped

½ cup raw long-grain
  converted rice
1 teaspoon salt
½ teaspoon leaf basil
  Dash pepper
4 slices American cheese,
  cut into triangles

Place all ingredients except cheese triangles in Crock-Pot. Stir thoroughly to mix ground beef with other ingredients. Place 4 cheese triangles on top. Cover and cook on Low setting for 8 to 10 hours.

Before serving, top with remaining 4 cheese triangles.

4 servings (about 2 quarts).

Chuckwagon Venison: Substitute ground venison for the beef.

Jenny Joe's

2 lb. lean ground beef
1 medium onion, chopped
1 teaspoon salt
¼ teaspoon pepper
1 can (10¾ oz.) condensed
  chicken gumbo soup

¼ cup ketchup
1 tablespoon prepared
  mustard
8 toasted hamburger rolls

In skillet, brown ground beef; drain well. Combine all ingredients except hamburger rolls in Crock-Pot; stir well. Cover and cook on Low setting for 6 to 9 hours (on High setting for 2 to 3 hours).

Serve spooned over toasted hamburger rolls.

8 servings (about 2 quarts).

Taverns

2½ lb. lean ground beef
1 large onion, chopped
1 cup ketchup
1 teaspoon chili powder
1 teaspoon dry mustard
1 teaspoon salt
2 cups beef broth or water
Toasted hamburger rolls

In skillet, brown ground beef; drain well. Place browned beef and remaining ingredients except hamburger rolls in Crock-Pot; stir well. Cover and cook on Low setting for 8 to 12 hours.

Taste for seasoning before serving. Serve spooned over toasted hamburger rolls.

6 to 8 servings (about 2 quarts).

Simple Stroganoff

1½ lb. lean ground beef
½ cup flour
½ cup chopped onion
1 cup cream-style cottage cheese
1 can (6 oz.) tomato paste
1 tablespoon Worcestershire sauce
1½ teaspoons salt
1 teaspoon oregano
¼ teaspoon garlic powder
Dash pepper
1 can (4 oz.) sliced mushrooms, drained
1 can (14 oz.) beef broth or 2 cups meat stock

In skillet, brown ground beef, flour and onion; drain well. Place in Crock-Pot.

Whip cottage cheese until smooth; add tomato paste and seasonings. Mix well and add to meat mixture with mushrooms and beef broth. Stir until slightly blended. Cover and cook on Low setting for 6 to 8 hours.

4 to 6 servings (about 2½ quarts).

Layered Beef 'n Potatoes

1 lb. ground beef	Dash pepper
1 can (8 oz.) tomato sauce and bits	1½ cups dried mashed potato flakes
1 can (12 oz.) Mexicorn, drained	1½ cups sour cream
1 tablespoon instant minced onion	⅓ cup water
1 teaspoon salt	1½ cups grated process American cheese

In skillet, brown ground beef; drain well. Place in Crock-Pot and add tomato sauce, corn, onion, salt and pepper; mix well. In bowl, mix potato flakes with sour cream and water. Spread potato mixture over beef. Top with grated cheese. Cover and cook on Low setting for 7 to 10 hours.

4 servings (about 2½ quarts).

Alamo Tamale Supper

2 cans (15 oz. each) beef tamales	1 can (8 oz.) tomato sauce
1 medium onion, finely chopped	1 teaspoon chili powder
1 can (8 oz.) whole-kernel corn, drained	1 cup grated sharp process cheese
	¼ cup sliced, pitted ripe olives

Slice tamales in half crosswise and arrange in bottom of greased Crock-Pot. Sprinkle chopped onion over tamales. Add corn. Mix tomato sauce and chili powder; pour into Crock-Pot. Top with grated cheese and sprinkle with sliced ripe olives. Cover and cook on Low setting for 5 to 7 hours (on High setting for 2 hours).

4 servings (about 1½ quarts). Double recipe for 5-quart Crock-Pot.

Beef Tacos with Mexican Sauce

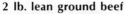

2 lb. lean ground beef
2 medium onions, finely chopped
1 to 2 tablespoons chili powder
1 teaspoon leaf oregano
1 teaspoon paprika
2 teaspoons salt
⅓ cup taco sauce

1 tablespoon Worcestershire sauce
1 can (16 oz.) pinto beans or green peas, drained and pureed in blender
Taco shells
Mexican Sauce (below)

In large skillet, brown ground beef and onions; drain well. Place beef and onions in Crock-Pot. Stir in remaining ingredients except taco shells and Mexican Sauce. Cover and cook on Low setting for 8 to 10 hours. Taste for seasoning. Fill taco shells and serve with sauce.

Fills 2 to 3 dozen taco shells (about 2½ quarts).

NOTE: This taco filling freezes beautifully.

MEXICAN SAUCE

2 cups chopped peeled tomatoes or 1 can (16 oz.) whole tomatoes
1 small onion, quartered
1 clove garlic

1 tablespoon chili powder
½ teaspoon leaf oregano
1 teaspoon salt
1 small jalapeño pepper, fresh or canned (optional)

Combine all ingredients in blender container; blend until smooth. Pour into small saucepan; simmer for 30 minutes.

About 3½ cups.

Veal Steak in Sour Cream

1½-lb. veal round steak
¼ cup flour
1 teaspoon salt
1 tablespoon paprika
Dash pepper
1 tablespoon dried parsley
   flakes
1 large onion, finely
   chopped
2 cloves garlic, minced
   (optional)

2 beef bouillon cubes
1 cup boiling water
2 large ripe tomatoes,
   peeled and chopped,
   or 1 cup canned
   whole tomatoes
½ cup sour cream
3 tablespoons flour

Trim all excess fat from veal, remove bone and cut meat into 1½-inch cubes. Combine ¼ cup flour, the salt, paprika, pepper and parsley flakes and toss with veal in Crock-Pot to coat thoroughly. Add onion and garlic. Dissolve beef bouillon cubes in boiling water; stir into Crock-Pot with tomatoes. Cover and cook on Low setting for 8 to 10 hours. During last hour, combine sour cream with 3 tablespoons flour and pour into Crock-Pot; stir well. Before serving, taste for seasoning.

4 servings (about 2 quarts).

AUTOMATIC TIMING

An 8-hour workday needn't restrict your choices to "all-day" recipes. Team up your Crock-Pot with an automatic timer and you have the solution. Simply prepare your chosen recipe and cover the pot. Set the automatic timer for the desired cooking span and go off about your business. (Caution: Be sure the food is chilled—and don't delay the starting time for more than 2 hours.) Remember, too, after the timer turns the Crock-Pot off, your dish will remain at the proper serving temperature for up to 2 hours.

Veal Ragout

3- to 4-lb. veal breast	2 teaspoons salt
1 onion, chopped	2 cups water
1 carrot, pared and sliced	Sauce (below)
1 stalk celery, sliced	1 cup heavy cream
1 bay leaf	1 egg, lightly beaten

Trim all excess fat from veal. Place veal and chopped vegetables in Crock-Pot; add remaining ingredients except Sauce, cream and egg. Cover and cook on Low setting for 7 to 9 hours. Refrigerate cooked veal and broth in container. Chill until fat rises to top and can easily be removed. Remove meat from bones and cut into 1-inch cubes. (There should be about 3½ cups veal.) Remove 2 cups broth for sauce.

One to 3 hours before serving, prepare Sauce. Combine Sauce and cubed veal in Crock-Pot. Cover and cook on High setting for 2 to 3 hours to allow flavors to blend. Thirty minutes before serving, combine heavy cream and egg; stir into Crock-Pot. Serve with small onions and carrots simmered on top of range in ½ cup veal stock.

8 servings (about 2½ quarts).

SAUCE

⅓ cup butter or margarine	⅓ cup flour
½ pound fresh mushrooms, sliced	2 cups veal broth
	½ cup dry white wine

On top of range (or in microwave oven using 2-quart glass casserole), melt butter in medium-size saucepan over medium heat. Stir in mushrooms and sauté lightly. Add flour, stirring constantly; stir in broth and wine. Cook and stir until thickened.

Roast Pork

3- to 4-lb. pork loin roast,
    well trimmed
Kitchen Bouquet
Garlic salt
Salt and pepper

3 to 4 sweet potatoes or
    baking potatoes, whole
    (peeled or unpeeled)

Brush pork roast well with Kitchen Bouquet. Sprinkle with garlic salt, salt and pepper. Place potatoes in bottom of Crock-Pot. Place pork roast on "rack" of potatoes. Cover and cook on Low setting 10 to 12 hours.

4 to 6 servings (about 3 quarts).

Apple-Glazed Pork Roast

3- to 4-lb. pork loin roast,
    well trimmed
Salt and pepper
4 to 6 apples, cored and
    quartered

¼ cup apple juice
3 tablespoons brown sugar
1 teaspoon ground ginger

Rub roast with salt and pepper. Brown pork roast under broiler to remove excess fat; drain well. Place apple quarters in bottom of Crock-Pot. Place roast on top of apples. Combine apple juice, brown sugar and ginger. Spoon over top surface of roast, moistening well. Cover and cook on Low setting for 10 to 12 hours or until done.

6 to 8 servings (about 3 quarts).

Mexican Pork Roast

2 medium onions, chopped
2 carrots, pared and sliced
3- to 4½-lb. pork loin or
    shoulder roast
2 teaspoons salt

½ teaspoon leaf oregano
½ teaspoon cumin seed
½ teaspoon coriander
2 cups water

Place onions and carrots in Crock-Pot. Rub pork roast with seasonings. Place on top of vegetables; add water. Cover and cook on Low setting for 10 to 12 hours.

Good when shredded and served in hot buttered tortillas with spicy taco sauce.

6 to 8 servings (about 3½ quarts).

Braised Pork

3- to 4-lb. pork loin roast,
    well trimmed
3 cloves garlic, slivered
    Salt and pepper
½ teaspoon sage

1 cup chicken broth
½ cup dry vermouth
¼ cup pimiento-stuffed
    olives, sliced
¼ cup flour

Brown pork roast under broiler to remove excess fat; drain well. Insert garlic slivers in roast and season lightly with salt, pepper and sage. Place browned pork roast in Crock-Pot. Add remaining ingredients except flour. Cover and cook on Low setting for 10 to 12 hours. Remove roast. In small bowl, combine flour with ½ cup gravy juices from Crock-Pot. Turn to High setting and stir in flour paste. Cook and stir until thickened. Serve sauce over pork, with regular or saffron rice.

8 servings (about 3 quarts).

Stuffed Pork Chops

4 double pork loin chops,
well trimmed
Salt and pepper
1 can (12 oz.) whole-kernel
corn, drained
1 small onion, chopped
1 small green pepper,
seeded and chopped

1 cup fresh bread crumbs
½ teaspoon leaf oregano or
leaf sage
⅓ cup raw long-grain
converted rice
1 can (8 oz.) tomato sauce

Cut a pocket in each chop, cutting from the edge almost to the bone. Lightly season pockets with salt and pepper. In bowl, combine all ingredients except pork chops and tomato sauce. Pack vegetable mixture into pockets. Secure along fat side with wooden picks.

Pour any remaining vegetable mixture into Crock-Pot. Moisten top surface of each chop with tomato sauce. Add stuffed pork chops to Crock-Pot, stacking to fit if necessary. Pour any remaining tomato sauce on top. Cover and cook on Low setting for 8 to 10 hours or until done.

To serve, remove chops to heatproof platter and mound vegetable-rice mixture in center.

4 servings (about 3 quarts).

Spicy Pork and Cabbage

4 to 6 pork loin chops
(about 1 inch thick),
well trimmed
Salt and pepper
Kitchen Bouquet
4 cups coarsely shredded
cabbage
3 to 4 tart apples, cored
and diced

½ small onion, chopped
2 whole cloves
½ small bay leaf
¼ cup sugar
1 cup water
2 tablespoons cider vinegar
2 teaspoons salt

Season pork chops lightly with salt and pepper and brush with Kitchen Bouquet; set aside. Place cabbage, apples and onion in Crock-Pot. Add remaining ingredients except pork chops. Toss together well to evenly distribute spices. Arrange chops on top of cabbage mixture, stacking to fit. Cover and cook on Low setting for 8 to 10 hours (on High setting for 2 to 3 hours).

4 to 6 servings (about 3½ quarts).

Fruited Pork Chops

6 pork loin chops
(about 1 inch thick),
well trimmed
2 tablespoons cooking oil
Salt

6 tart apples, cored and
thickly sliced
¼ cup dried currants
1 tablespoon lemon juice
¼ cup brown sugar

In skillet, brown chops in oil. Sprinkle with salt during browning; drain well. Place chops in Crock-Pot. Combine remaining ingredients and pour over chops. Cover and cook on Low setting for 7 to 9 hours.

6 servings (about 2½ quarts).

Pork Chops and Apple Slices

4 pork loin chops (about
1 inch thick), well
trimmed
2 medium apples, peeled,
cored and sliced

1 teaspoon butter
¼ teaspoon nutmeg
(optional)
Salt and pepper

In skillet, brown pork chops quickly; drain well. Arrange a layer of sliced apples in Crock-Pot, then a layer of pork chops; repeat. Dot with butter; sprinkle with nutmeg. Add salt and pepper. Cover and cook on Low setting for 7 to 9 hours.

4 servings (about 2½ quarts).

Pork and Veal with Sauerkraut

1 can (16 oz.) sauerkraut
1 lb. veal, cut into 1½-inch
cubes
1 lb. pork, well trimmed
and cut into 1½-inch
cubes
1 can (16 oz.) tomato
wedges

½ to 1 teaspoon caraway
seed
1 cup sour cream
¼ cup flour
2 teaspoons salt
⅛ teaspoon pepper

Rinse sauerkraut under cold water; drain well. Combine sauerkraut, veal, pork, tomato wedges and caraway seed in Crock-Pot; stir well. Cover and cook on Low setting for 8 to 12 hours.

One hour before serving, combine sour cream, flour, salt and pepper. Stir gently into Crock-Pot. Cover and cook until thickened.

6 servings (about 2½ quarts).

Chop Suey

2 to 3 pork shoulder
chops, boned, well
trimmed and diced
2 cups cubed cooked or
raw chicken
½ cup chicken broth
1 cup diagonally sliced
celery

2 teaspoons soy sauce
½ teaspoon sugar
Salt
1½ cups water chestnuts,
thinly sliced
1½ cups bamboo shoots,
in julienne strips

Combine all ingredients in Crock-Pot; stir well. Cover and
cook on Low setting for 8 to 10 hours (on High setting for
4 to 5 hours). If desired, thicken sauce with a cornstarch-
water paste just before serving.

4 servings (about 2 quarts). Double recipe for 5-quart Crock-
Pot.

Mexican Carnitas

1 lb. lean boneless pork,
cut into small cubes
½ teaspoon monosodium
glutamate
1 package (10 oz.) frozen
French-style green
beans, partially thawed

2 tablespoons minced
onion
2 tablespoons chopped
pimiento
½ teaspoon seasoned salt
⅛ teaspoon pepper

Sprinkle pork cubes with monosodium glutamate and toss
lightly. Place green beans in Crock-Pot. Top with onion,
pimiento, seasoned salt and pepper; add cubed pork. Cover and
cook on Low setting for 7 to 9 hours.

3 to 4 servings (about 1½ quarts). Double recipe for 5-quart
Crock-Pot.

Chili Verde

2 lb. extra-lean boneless
    pork, cut into 1-inch
    cubes
1 lb. boneless beef chuck,
    cut into 1-inch cubes
1 large green pepper,
    seeded and chopped
2 cloves garlic, minced
1 can (28 oz.) whole
    tomatoes, mashed
1 can (4 oz.) green chili
    peppers, drained,
    seeded and chopped

⅓ cup chopped parsley or
    2 tablespoons dried
    parsley flakes
1 teaspoon sugar
2 teaspoons cumin seed or
    1 tablespoon ground
    cumin
2 whole cloves
½ cup beef broth

Combine all ingredients in Crock-Pot; stir thoroughly. Cover and cook on Low setting for 8 to 10 hours.

Before serving, taste for seasoning and add salt and more cumin if needed.

6 to 8 servings (about 3 quarts).

Cantonese Sweet-Sour Pork

2-lb. lean pork shoulder,
    cut into strips
1 green pepper, seeded
    and cut into strips
½ medium onion, thinly
    sliced
¼ cup brown sugar
    (packed)

2 tablespoons cornstarch
2 cups pineapple chunks
    (reserve juice)
¼ cup cider vinegar
¼ cup water
1 tablespoon soy sauce
½ teaspoon salt
    Chow mein noodles

Place pork strips in Crock-Pot. Add green pepper and sliced onion. In bowl, mix brown sugar and cornstarch. Add 1 cup reserved pineapple juice, the vinegar, water, soy sauce and salt; blend until smooth. Pour over meat and vegetables. Cover and cook on Low setting for 7 to 9 hours.

One hour before serving, add pineapple chunks; stir into meat and sauce.

Serve over chow mein noodles.

4 to 6 servings (about 2½ quarts).

Pork Subgum

1 lb. lean boneless pork, cubed and browned
1 medium onion, chopped
1 medium green pepper, seeded and cut into ¼-inch strips
2 cans (4 oz. each) sliced mushrooms, drained
1 can (7 oz.) water chestnuts, drained and sliced

½-inch strip crystallized ginger or 1 teaspoon ground ginger
1 cup chicken broth
1 tablespoon soy sauce
Salt and pepper
1 can (16 oz.) Chinese vegetables, drained
3 tablespoons cornstarch
3 tablespoons water
Chow mein noodles

Combine all ingredients except Chinese vegetables, cornstarch, water and chow mein noodles in Crock-Pot; stir well. Cover and cook on Low setting for 8 to 10 hours (on High setting for 4 to 5 hours).

One hour before serving, turn to High setting and stir in Chinese vegetables. Combine cornstarch and water and add to Crock-Pot. Taste for seasoning. Cover and continue cooking until thickened.

Serve over chow mein noodles.

4 to 6 servings (about 2 quarts). Double recipe for 5-quart Crock-Pot.

Candied Polynesian Spareribs

2 lb. lean pork spareribs
⅓ cup soy sauce
1 tablespoon ground
   ginger
¼ cup cornstarch
½ cup cider vinegar
1 cup sugar

¼ cup water
1 tablespoon salt
½ teaspoon dry mustard
1 small piece gingerroot or
   crystallized ginger
   (about 1 inch)

Cut spareribs into individual 3-inch pieces. Mix soy sauce, ground ginger and cornstarch until smooth; brush mixture over spareribs. Place ribs on rack of broiler pan. Bake in preheated 425° oven for 20 minutes to remove fat; drain. Combine remaining ingredients in Crock-Pot; stir well. Add browned ribs. Cover and cook on Low setting for 8 to 10 hours.

If desired, brown and crisp ribs in broiler for 10 minutes before serving.

4 servings (about 2½ quarts).

Honey Ribs and Rice

2 lb. extra-lean back ribs
1 can (10½ oz.) condensed
   beef consommé
½ cup water
2 tablespoons maple
   syrup

2 tablespoons honey
3 tablespoons soy sauce
2 tablespoons barbecue
   sauce
½ teaspoon dry mustard
1½ cups quick-cooking rice

If ribs are fat, place on broiler rack and broil for 15 to 20 minutes; drain well. Otherwise, wash ribs and pat dry. Cut ribs into single servings. Combine remaining ingredients except rice in Crock-Pot; stir to mix. Add ribs. Cover and cook on Low setting for 8 to 10 hours (on High setting for 4 to 5 hours).

Remove ribs and keep warm. Turn Crock-Pot to High setting; add 1½ cups quick-cooking rice and cook until done.

Serve rice on warm platter surrounded by ribs.

4 servings (about 2 quarts).

Baked Ham with Mustard Glaze

3- to 5-lb. canned ham, drained
10 to 12 whole cloves
½ cup brown sugar
1 tablespoon prepared mustard

2 teaspoons lemon juice
2 tablespoons orange juice
2 tablespoons cornstarch

Score fat on ham in a diamond pattern and stud with cloves. Place in Crock-Pot. Combine brown sugar, mustard and lemon juice and spoon on ham. Cover and cook on High setting 1 hour, then on Low setting for 6 to 7 hours or until ham is hot.

Remove ham to warm serving platter. Turn Crock-Pot to High setting. Combine orange juice and cornstarch to form a smooth paste. Stir into drippings in Crock-Pot. Cook, stirring occasionally until sauce is thickened. Spoon over ham.

5 or 6 quart unit: If cooking larger ham, cook 1 hour on High setting, then Low setting 8 to 10 hours.

12 to 15 servings.

Ham 'n Cola

½ cup brown sugar
1 teaspoon dry mustard
1 teaspoon prepared
    horseradish

¼ cup cola-type soft drink
3- to 4-lb. precooked ham

Thoroughly combine brown sugar, mustard and horseradish. Moisten with just enough cola to make a smooth paste; reserve remaining cola. Rub entire ham with mixture. Place ham in Crock-Pot and add remaining cola. Cover and cook on High setting for 1 hour, then turn to Low setting for 6 to 7 hours.

9 to 12 servings (about 3 quarts).

NOTE: A 5-lb. ham may be used in the 5-quart Crock-Pot. Cook on High setting 1 hour, then on Low setting for 8 to 10 hours.

Smoked Ham with Oranges

2 to 3 sweet potatoes,
    peeled and thinly
    sliced (¼ inch thick)
1 large smoked ham slice
    (about 1 inch thick),
    cut into serving pieces
3 seedless oranges, peeled
    and sliced

3 tablespoons frozen
    orange juice concen-
    trate, thawed
3 tablespoons honey
⅓ cup brown sugar
2 tablespoons cornstarch

Place sweet potatoes in Crock-Pot. Arrange ham and orange slices on sweet potatoes. Combine remaining ingredients; stir until consistency of a thin paste. Lightly spread over ham and oranges. Cover and cook on Low setting for 7 to 10 hours.

4 servings (about 2½ quarts).

Ham-Burger Balls with Yams

2 cups ground ham (about ½ lb.)
½ lb. ground chuck
1 cup whole wheat bread crumbs
1 egg, beaten
¼ cup minced onion
2 tablespoons salted sunflower seeds or ½ teaspoon salt

2 cans (23 oz. each) yams, drained and cut into cubes
½ cup dark corn syrup
½ cup apple juice or pineapple juice
¼ teaspoon nutmeg
1 to 2 tablespoons cornstarch

Thoroughly mix ground meats, bread crumbs, egg, onion and sunflower seeds. Shape into 12 to 16 meatballs. Place on rack in broiler pan. Bake meatballs in preheated 425° oven for 15 minutes.

Place yams in Crock-Pot. Combine corn syrup, juice and nutmeg and pour half over the yams. Place browned meatballs over yams and top with remaining sauce. Cover and cook on Low setting for 5 to 6 hours.

Transfer meatballs to serving dish; place yams in serving bowl and keep warm. Stir cornstarch into sauce. Cover and cook on High setting until thickened; pour over yams before serving.

4 to 6 servings (about 3 quarts).

A NOTE ABOUT PORK

Because fat can cause your dish to overcook and lose flavor, be sure your pork choice is well trimmed. Pre-brown ribs, roasts and other fatty cuts by broiling for 20 minutes; drain well. If using chops, choose 1-inch-thick loin chops (rib chops are too fat and too small to cook satisfactorily).

Ham Tetrazzini

1 can (10¾ oz.)
  condensed cream of
  mushroom soup
½ cup evaporated or
  scalded milk
1½ teaspoons prepared
  horseradish
½ cup grated Romano or
  Parmesan cheese
1 to 1½ cups cubed
  cooked ham

½ cup stuffed olives, sliced
  (optional)
1 can (4 oz.) sliced mushrooms, drained
¼ cup dry sherry or dry
  white wine
1 package (5 oz.)
  spaghetti
2 tablespoons butter,
  melted

Combine all ingredients except spaghetti and butter in Crock-Pot; stir well. Cover and cook on Low setting for 6 to 8 hours.

Just before serving, cook spaghetti according to package directions; drain and toss with butter. Stir into Crock-Pot. Sprinkle additional grated cheese over top.

4 servings (about 2 quarts). This recipe may be doubled for the 5-quart Crock-Pot.

Ham and Turnip Bake

5 cups diced turnips
2 cups coarsely ground
  cooked ham
1 cup finely chopped
  onion
1 cup finely chopped
  celery
½ cup finely chopped
  green pepper

1 egg
3 tablespoons butter or
  margarine, melted
½ cup fresh bread crumbs
  Salt and pepper
1 cup grated process
  American cheese

Cook diced turnips in 1 inch of boiling water for about 15 minutes or until tender; drain and mash. Add remaining ingredients except cheese. Pour into lightly greased Crock-Pot. Cover and cook on High setting for 2 to 4 hours (on Low setting for 4 to 8 hours). Before serving, sprinkle with grated cheese.

4 servings (about 2 quarts).

NOTE: Ground cooked chicken, turkey or beef may be substituted for the ham.

Ham and Cheese Supper

2 cups ground cooked ham
  (about ½ lb.)
½ cup finely crushed
  cheese crackers
1 egg
⅓ cup barbecue sauce
4 large potatoes, peeled
  and thinly sliced
1 medium onion, thinly
  sliced

2 tablespoons butter
2 tablespoons vegetable
  oil
⅔ cup evaporated milk
1 cup grated mozzarella
  cheese
1 teaspoon salt
¼ teaspoon paprika
⅛ teaspoon pepper

Combine ground ham, crushed crackers, egg and barbecue sauce and shape into 6 patties. In a skillet, sauté potato and onion slices in butter and oil over medium heat, turning frequently to prevent browning. Drain and place in Crock-Pot.

Combine milk, cheese and seasonings and pour over potatoes and onions. Layer ham patties on top. Cover and cook on Low setting for 3 to 5 hours.

6 servings (about 3 quarts).

Cranberry Canadian Bacon

4 lb. fully cooked Canadian bacon, unsliced	1 cup whole or jellied cranberry sauce

Remove casing from Canadian bacon. Place bacon in Crock-Pot, cutting to fit if necessary. Stir cranberry sauce and spoon over bacon. Cover and cook on High setting for 1 hour, then turn to Low setting for 6 to 7 hours.

Remove bacon from sauce; cut into ½-inch-thick slices. Arrange bacon on heatproof platter and spoon sauce over top. Broil for 10 to 15 minutes to glaze.

12 to 16 servings (about 2½ quarts).

Sausage and Cheese Casserole

1 lb. bulk sausage	3 cups uncooked noodles
2 chicken bouillon cubes	½ green pepper, chopped
2 cups boiling water	1 small onion, chopped
¼ cup flour	2 carrots, pared and grated
2 tablespoons butter	1 jar (2 oz.) pimiento,
4 oz. bleu cheese, crumbled	drained

In skillet, brown sausage; drain well. In large bowl, dissolve chicken bouillon cubes in boiling water; add flour, butter and bleu cheese and mix until smooth (or process in blender a few seconds). Stir sausage, noodles and vegetables into sauce and pour into greased Crock-Pot. Cover and cook on Low setting for 5 to 7 hours.

4 to 6 servings (about 2½ quarts).

NOTE: Cooking time may be extended to 8 hours if the noodles are cooked separately until barely tender, drained and tossed in a small amount of oil. Reduce water to 1 cup.

Polish Sausage and Cabbage

½ head cabbage, coarsely
  sliced or shredded
1 small potato, peeled
  and diced
1 teaspoon salt
½ teaspoon caraway seed
  (optional)

1 large onion, thinly
  sliced
1½ lb. Polish sausage, cut
  into 1-inch pieces
1 can (14 oz.) chicken
  broth

Place sliced cabbage in Crock-Pot. Toss with diced potato, salt and caraway seed. Add sliced onion and Polish sausage. Pour chicken broth over all; stir lightly. Cover and cook on Low setting for 8 to 10 hours (on High setting for 2 to 4 hours).

This dish is delicious served with mustard, horseradish and boiled new potatoes.

4 servings (about 3½ quarts).

Bologna-'Baga Bake

1½ lb. ring bologna, sliced
3 large potatoes, peeled
   and diced
1 small rutabaga, peeled
   and diced

1 medium onion, chopped
Salt and pepper
4 cups water
½ to ¾ cup milk
Butter

Combine all ingredients except milk and butter in Crock-Pot; mix well. Cover and cook on Low setting for 8 to 10 hours (on High setting for 3 to 4 hours).

Remove bologna and drain liquid from Crock-Pot. Mash vegetables, adding milk. Mix meat into mashed vegetables. Serve hot, topped with butter.

4 servings (about 2½ quarts).

Italian Stew

1 cup broken spaghetti
1 tablespoon vegetable oil
2 beef bouillon cubes
2½ cups boiling water
6 large frankfurters,
   halved lengthwise and
   then crosswise

½ lb. small zucchini,
   thinly sliced
¼ cup tomato paste
½ teaspoon leaf oregano
¼ teaspoon leaf basil
1 teaspoon sugar

Cook spaghetti according to package directions until barely tender; drain. Toss with oil. Dissolve bouillon cubes in boiling water. Combine all ingredients in Crock-Pot; stir well. Cover and cook on Low setting for 6 to 8 hours.

6 servings (about 1½ quarts).

NOTE: Two cans (16 oz. each) zucchini may be substituted for the fresh zucchini; add during last hour of cooking.

The Babysitter's Favorite

3 cups sliced peeled apples	½ teaspoon salt
1 can (16 oz.) sweet potatoes, sliced	¼ teaspoon cinnamon
	¼ teaspoon nutmeg
1 lb. frankfurters, halved lengthwise	¼ teaspoon grated lemon rind
½ cup brown sugar	1 tablespoon butter

Place half of the apples, sweet potatoes and frankfurters in greased Crock-Pot. Combine sugar, salt, spices and lemon rind; sprinkle half of the mixture into Crock-Pot. Add remaining apples, sweet potatoes and frankfurters. Top with remaining spice mixture. Dot with butter. Cover and cook on Low setting for 2 to 9 hours.

6 to 8 servings (about 2 quarts).

Camp-Out Chili Dogs

1 lb. frankfurters	1 teaspoon chili powder
1 large onion, finely chopped, or 3 tablespoons dried minced onion	¼ lb. Cheddar cheese, cubed or grated
	Frankfurter rolls
2 cans (15 oz.) chili with beans	

Combine all ingredients except cheese and rolls in Crock-Pot; stir well. Cover and cook on Low setting for 5 to 10 hours (on High setting for 2 to 3 hours).

Add cheese just before serving and allow to melt slightly. Serve each frankfurter in a roll and spoon sauce over top.

6 to 8 servings (about 2 quarts).

Stuffed Lamb Shoulder

3- to 4-lb. lamb shoulder,
  boned
½ lb. bulk sausage
1 medium onion, chopped
1 tablespoon dried parsley
  flakes
½ teaspoon leaf marjoram
½ teaspoon leaf basil

½ teaspoon leaf oregano
1 clove garlic, minced
  (optional)
1 onion, sliced
2 stalks celery, sliced
2 carrots, pared and sliced
  Kitchen Bouquet
  Salt and pepper

Trim all excess fat from lamb shoulder. To prepare stuffing, brown sausage and chopped onion in skillet; drain well. Stir in herbs and garlic. Stuff lamb with mixture. Roll lamb and fasten with skewers or string. Place sliced onion, celery and carrots in Crock-Pot. Place stuffed and rolled lamb on top of vegetables. Rub top of lamb with Kitchen Bouquet; sprinkle with salt and pepper. Cover and cook on High setting for 1 hour, then turn to Low setting for 10 to 12 hours.

Serve lamb sliced, with the natural juices poured over vegetables and meat.

6 to 8 servings (about 3½ quarts).

Lamb Chops with Orange Sauce

8 lamb rib chops
2 tablespoons vegetable
  oil
½ cup orange juice

2 tablespoons honey
2 teaspoons salt
2 tablespoons cornstarch
1 teaspoon grated orange
  peel

In skillet, brown lamb chops in oil; drain well. Thoroughly combine orange juice, honey, salt, cornstarch and grated orange peel. Brush browned lamb chops with orange mixture and place in Crock-Pot. Cover and cook on Low setting for 6 to 8 hours.

If a thicker sauce is desired, remove chops before serving and turn to High setting; stir in a mixture of 2 tablespoons cornstarch and ¼ cup water. Cook, stirring, until the sauce is transparent.

4 servings (about 2½ quarts).

German Lamb in Sour Cream

2 lb. lean boneless lamb, cut into 1-inch cubes	¼ teaspoon leaf rosemary
2 tablespoons vegetable oil	1 large onion, chopped
	1½ cups beef broth
½ cup flour	1 teaspoon tarragon vinegar
2 teaspoons salt	2 tablespoons flour
½ teaspoon dill seed	2 tablespoons water
½ teaspoon caraway seed	1 cup sour cream

If lamb is fat, brown in oil in skillet; drain well. Combine ½ cup flour with salt, dill seed, caraway seed and rosemary; toss with lamb cubes to coat thoroughly. Place lamb cubes in lightly oiled Crock-Pot. Stir in remaining ingredients except the 2 tablespoons flour, water and sour cream. Cover and cook on Low setting for 10 to 14 hours.

Thirty minutes before serving, turn to High setting. Combine the 2 tablespoons flour with water; stir into Crock-Pot. Cover and cook until thickened. Stir in sour cream.

Serve lamb over hot buttered noodles and garnish with additional sour cream.

4 to 6 servings (about 2 quarts).

Ragout of Lamb

3 lb. lean boneless lamb,
    cut into 1-inch cubes
¼ cup flour
1½ teaspoons salt
    Dash pepper
2 tablespoons vegetable
    oil
1½ cups chicken broth
1 clove garlic, peeled and
    crushed (optional)

¼ teaspoon leaf marjoram
¼ teaspoon leaf savory
2 tablespoons dried
    parsley flakes
1 tablespoon lemon juice
1 teaspoon freshly grated
    lemon peel

Pat lamb cubes dry with absorbent towels. Combine flour, salt and pepper and toss with the lamb cubes. In large skillet, brown lamb in oil; drain well. Place browned cubes in Crock-Pot and stir in remaining ingredients. Cover and cook on Low setting for 8 to 10 hours (on High setting for 3 to 4½ hours). Serve over hot buttered noodles.

6 servings (about 2½ quarts).

Lamb Stew with Vegetables

3 lb. boneless lamb
    stewing meat, well
    trimmed
½ cup flour
2 teaspoons salt
1 teaspoon sugar
½ teaspoon leaf thyme
¼ teaspoon pepper
¼ teaspoon garlic powder
    (optional)

1 can (14 oz.) beef broth
3 to 4 potatoes, peeled
    and cubed
3 large carrots, pared and
    thinly sliced
6 to 8 small white onions
1 package (10 oz.) frozen
    peas

Wipe off any collected juices from lamb. Combine flour with salt, sugar, thyme, pepper and garlic powder; toss with lamb to coat thoroughly. Place all ingredients except peas in Crock-Pot; stir well. Cover and cook on Low setting for 10 to 12 hours.

One hour before serving, turn to High setting and stir in frozen peas. Cover and cook until done.

6 to 8 servings (about 3½ quarts).

NOTE: Peas may be added at beginning of cooking, but will darken slightly.

Grecian Lamb Stew

3 lb. lean boneless lamb, cut into 1-inch cubes	1 teaspoon crystallized ginger
¼ cup flour	¼ teaspoon saffron threads
2 teaspoons salt	½ cup beef broth
¼ teaspoon pepper	1 can (16 oz.) whole tomatoes
2 medium onions, chopped	
2 cloves garlic, minced	1 cup raisins
1 bay leaf (whole)	⅔ cup blanched almonds
¼ cup chopped parsley or 2 tablespoons dried parsley flakes	1 tablespoon butter or margarine
	Minced parsley

Place cubed lamb in Crock-Pot. Add flour, salt, pepper, onions and garlic; mix thoroughly. Add remaining ingredients except almonds, butter and minced parsley; stir well. Cover and cook on Low setting for 8 to 12 hours (on High setting for 3 to 4 hours). Taste for seasoning. In small skillet, toast almonds in butter until golden brown. Serve stew sprinkled with toasted almonds and minced parsley.

6 servings (about 3 quarts).

Savory Lamb Riblets

3 lb. lamb breast, cut up
Salt and pepper
1 cup barbecue sauce
2 tablespoons frozen
    orange juice concen-
    trate, thawed

2 tablespoons dried parsley
    flakes
¼ teaspoon leaf rosemary

Place lamb breast on broiler rack of broiler pan; sprinkle with salt and pepper. Broil for 20 minutes or until brown; drain well. Combine barbecue sauce with remaining ingredients. Coat lamb well with mixture; place in Crock-Pot. Cover and cook on Low setting for 8 to 10 hours (on High setting for 4 to 5 hours).

Remove lamb from sauce. Place on large heatproof platter and spoon sauce over top. Place under broiler to crisp, if desired.

4 to 6 servings (about 3 quarts).

SUBSTITUTE TO SUIT

You can tailor any main-dish recipe to suit your own taste preferences. It's easy. Simply substitute liquids, condensed soups, seasonings or vegetables of your own choosing for the ones suggested in the recipes—providing, of course, the amounts are the same. Here are a few examples:

- Substitute beef or chicken broth for wine or sherry.
- Try cream of chicken soup instead of cream of celery.
- Hate tomatoes? Replace a 16-ounce can with 1 can of condensed cream soup plus 6 ounces of water.
- Use sliced celery instead of sliced onions or green pepper.
- Omit the seasonings—or add just before serving.

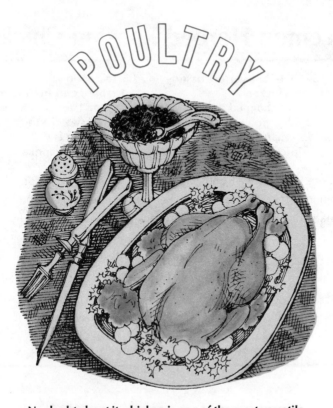

POULTRY

No doubt about it, chicken is one of the most versatile
menu stars around. Roast it whole, sauce the breasts,
casserole the pieces. And all in your Crock-Pot.
The delicate chicken flavor is steeped in—
never diluted, boiled away or sogged down.
Use these recipes as your starting point;
then with your own favorite combinations of herbs and sauces,
you can go in as many directions as a compass—
East, Continental or good old and new American.
While some recipes suggest browning (the chicken will be firmer),
it isn't absolutely essential. Try it both ways . . .
and you decide. But if you don't brown the chicken,
do rinse well and pat dry—
this gets rid of unneeded juices and package residue.

Lemon Herbed Roasted Chicken

3- to 4-lb. fryer or roasting
  chicken
¼ cup chopped onion
2 tablespoons butter or
  margarine
Juice of one lemon

½ teaspoon salt
1 tablespoon fresh parsley
  (or 1 teaspoon dried
  parsley flakes)
¼ teaspoon leaf thyme
¼ teaspoon paprika

Rinse chicken well and pat dry; remove any excess fat. Place onion in the cavity of the chicken and rub the skin with butter or margarine. Place chicken in Crock-Pot. Squeeze the juice of the lemon over the chicken and sprinkle with remaining seasonings. Cover and cook on Low setting 8 to 10 hours.

REMOVABLE STONEWARE

Foods may be prepared the night before and refrigerated in the stoneware bowl. A few hints to remember:

•Place stoneware bowl in heating base and turn on to desired setting. Bowl and food do not need to be allowed to come to room temperature. Use maximum cooking time.

•Do not preheat electrical base.

•If preparing dishes with rice or pasta, do not add liquid until just before cooking.

•Potatoes may be kept from darkening by rinsing in a solution of 1 cup water and ½ teaspoon cream of tartar. Drain and proceed as recipe directs.

"Fried" Chicken

2½- to 3-lb. fryer, cut into
   serving pieces
1 cup flour
1 teaspoon salt
⅛ teaspoon freshly ground
   pepper

¼ teaspoon garlic powder
1 teaspoon paprika
1 teaspoon leaf sage or
   oregano
Butter or vegetable oil

Rinse chicken pieces and pat dry. Combine flour with remaining ingredients except butter. Toss chicken pieces with
flour mixture to coat. In skillet, heat butter to ¼-inch depth
and cook chicken over medium-high heat until golden brown.
Place browned chicken in Crock-Pot, adding wings first; add
no liquid. Cover and cook on Low setting for 8 to 10 hours.

4 servings (about 3 quarts).

Chicken 'n Olives

3-lb. fryer, cut into serving
   pieces
Salt and pepper
1 clove garlic, minced
1 large onion, chopped
2 bay leaves

¾ cup beer
1 can (8 oz.) tomato sauce
½ cup pimiento-stuffed
   olives
Fluffy rice

Rinse chicken pieces and pat dry. Lightly season with salt
and pepper. Combine all ingredients except chicken and rice
in Crock-Pot; stir well. Add chicken pieces, coating well; be
sure all chicken is moistened. Cover and cook on Low setting for 7 to 9 hours.

   Serve chicken and sauce over hot fluffy rice.

4 to 6 servings (about 3 quarts).

Chicken 'n Rice in a Bag

3-lb. fryer, cut into serving pieces	⅔ cup water
1 cup raw long-grain converted rice	1 envelope (1½ oz.) dry onion soup mix
1 can (10¾ oz.) condensed cream of chicken soup	

Rinse chicken pieces and pat dry; set aside. Combine rice, cream of chicken soup and water in Crock-Pot; stir well to mix in soup. Place chicken pieces in a see-through roasting bag; add onion soup mix. Shake bag to coat chicken pieces thoroughly. Puncture 4 to 6 holes in bottom of bag. Fold top of bag over chicken and place in Crock-Pot on top of rice. Cover and cook on Low setting for 8 to 10 hours. Remove chicken pieces to warm platter. Serve with rice.

4 servings (about 3 quarts).

Hunter's Chicken

3-lb. fryer, cut into serving pieces	2 stalks celery, chopped
Garlic salt	1 can (4 oz.) sliced mushrooms, drained
Pepper	¼ cup dry sherry
Cinnamon	1 can (16 oz.) tomato wedges
1 medium green pepper, seeded and chopped	3 tablespoons flour
2 small onions, sliced	3 tablespoons water
	Hot spaghetti

Rinse chicken pieces and pat dry. Season with garlic salt, pepper and cinnamon. Place green pepper, onions and celery in Crock-Pot. Add seasoned chicken parts. Pour in mushrooms, sherry and tomatoes; stir well. Cover and cook on

Low setting for 8 to 10 hours.

Remove chicken pieces; bone and return meat to sauce. Make a smooth paste of flour and water; stir into Crock-Pot. Cover and cook on High setting for 15 to 30 minutes or until gravy is thickened. Serve over hot spaghetti.

6 servings (about 3 quarts).

International Chicken

3-lb. fryer, cut into serving pieces	2 cloves garlic, minced
¼ cup flour	½ cup raisins
2 teaspoons salt	1 can (16 oz.) whole tomatoes, mashed
2 teaspoons curry powder	3 tablespoons flour
⅛ teaspoon pepper	3 tablespoons water
1 large onion, chopped	
1 large green pepper, seeded and sliced into rings	

Rinse chicken pieces and pat dry. Combine ¼ cup flour, the salt, curry powder and pepper. Dust chicken well with flour mixture. Place coated chicken in Crock-Pot and mix in chopped vegetables, garlic and raisins. Pour tomatoes over all. Cover and cook on Low setting for 8 to 10 hours (on High setting for 3 to 4 hours).

Remove chicken pieces to warm platter. Thicken sauce before serving by stirring a smooth paste of the 3 tablespoons flour and water into the sauce in Crock-Pot. Cover and cook on High setting until sauce is thickened. This is good served on rice—especially saffron rice. Spoon sauce over top.

4 servings (about 2½ quarts).

Tomato-Chicken Risotto

3-lb. fryer, cut into serving
pieces, or 6 chicken
parts
½ lb. pork link sausage, cut
into chunks
Kitchen Bouquet
(optional)
1 small green pepper,
seeded and chopped

⅓ cup chopped onion
1 clove garlic, minced
2 cans (8 oz. each) tomato
sauce
½ cup water
1 teaspoon salt
1 cup raw long-grain
converted rice
Grated Parmesan cheese

Rinse chicken pieces and pat dry; set aside. In skillet, brown sausage. Remove with slotted spoon and drain on absorbent towels. Brown chicken pieces in sausage drippings; drain well. Lightly brush with Kitchen Bouquet. Place chicken in Crock-Pot. Combine drained sausage with remaining ingredients except cheese and pour over chicken. Cover and cook on Low setting for 8 to 10 hours.

Just before serving, sprinkle with grated Parmesan cheese.

6 servings (about 3 quarts).

Chicken Fricassee

3- to 4-lb. stewing chicken
or fryer, cut into
serving pieces
2 teaspoons salt
1 teaspoon paprika
2 medium onions, sliced
3 stalks celery, sliced
2 carrots, pared and sliced

1 bay leaf
1 cup chicken broth
½ cup flour
½ cup water
1 package (10 oz.) noodles,
cooked and drained
Chopped parsley

Rinse chicken pieces and pat dry. Season with salt and paprika. Place sliced vegetables and bay leaf in Crock-Pot.

Place chicken pieces on top of vegetables. Pour in chicken broth. Cover and cook on Low setting for 8 to 12 hours.

One hour before serving, turn to High setting. Remove chicken pieces; bone and return meat to Crock-Pot. Make a smooth paste of flour and water and stir into liquid in Crock-Pot. Cover and cook until thickened.

Serve over hot noodles; sprinkle with chopped parsley.

6 to 8 servings (about 3½ quarts).

Chicken Chow Mein

4-lb. hen or fryer, cut up	**1 can (5 or 6 oz.) bamboo**
2 cups water	**shoots (optional)**
2 large white onions,	**1 can (6 or 8½ oz.) water**
chopped	**chestnuts, drained and**
2 cups diagonally sliced	**sliced**
celery	**3 tablespoons molasses**
¼ cup flour or cornstarch	**Chow mein noodles or**
¼ cup soy sauce	**fluffy rice**
1 can (16 oz.) bean	**Toasted slivered almonds**
sprouts, drained	

Place chicken with water, onions and celery in Crock-Pot. Cover and cook on Low setting for 8 to 10 hours.

One hour before serving, turn to High setting. Remove chicken; bone and cut up meat into bite-size pieces. Return to Crock-Pot. Combine flour with soy sauce and stir into Crock-Pot with bean sprouts, bamboo shoots, water chestnuts and molasses. Stir well until thickened. Taste for seasoning. Turn to Low until ready to serve, up to 4 hours.

Serve over chow mein noodles or hot fluffy rice. Sprinkle with toasted slivered almonds.

8 to 10 servings (about 3½ quarts).

Chicken Tarragon

3-lb. fryer, cut into serving
pieces
⅓ cup flour
1 teaspoon salt
¼ teaspoon pepper
1 medium onion, sliced

½ teaspoon leaf tarragon
½ cup orange-flavored
breakfast drink powder
1 can (4 oz.) sliced mushrooms, undrained

Rinse chicken pieces and pat dry. Combine flour with salt
and pepper. Coat chicken with mixture. Separate onion slices
into rings and place in bottom of Crock-Pot. Add seasoned
chicken pieces. Sprinkle with tarragon. Stir orange drink
powder into mushrooms and add to Crock-Pot. Cover and
cook on Low setting for 8 to 10 hours.

4 to 6 servings (about 3 quarts).

Chicken Cassandra

3-lb. fryer, cut into
serving pieces
⅓ cup Italian salad
dressing
1½ cups raw long-grain
converted rice
2 cans (16 oz. each) stewed
tomatoes, chopped

⅓ cup dry white wine
1 teaspoon Italian
seasoning
⅛ teaspoon celery seed
1½ teaspoons salt
1 package (10 oz.) frozen
Brussels sprouts,
broken apart

Rinse chicken pieces and pat dry. In skillet, sauté chicken in
Italian salad dressing over medium heat. Mix rice, tomatoes,
wine, seasonings and Brussels sprouts in Crock-Pot. Top with
chicken. Cover and cook on Low setting for 7 to 9 hours.

8 servings (about 3 quarts).

Souper Chicken

2 lb. chicken parts
1 can (10¾ oz.) condensed
cream of celery soup
¼ cup flour
2 medium zucchini, cut
lengthwise, then sliced
diagonally into ½-inch
pieces

1 teaspoon paprika
½ teaspoon leaf basil
1 clove garlic, minced
1 cup drained canned
tomato wedges

Rinse chicken parts and pat dry. Mix celery soup with flour. Combine all ingredients in Crock-Pot; stir thoroughly to coat chicken. Cover and cook on Low setting for 8 to 10 hours.

4 servings (about 2½ quarts).

Chicken Lickin'

6 to 8 chicken legs, thighs
or breasts
3 tablespoons butter or
margarine
1 large onion, chopped
1 clove garlic, minced
1½ teaspoons salt
2 teaspoons paprika

½ teaspoon ground ginger
½ teaspoon chili powder
1 can (16 oz.) whole
tomatoes
1 can (4 oz.) sliced mushrooms, drained
½ cup heavy cream
(optional)

Rinse chicken parts and pat dry. In skillet, melt butter and brown chicken quickly on both sides. Place chicken in Crock-Pot. Stir together remaining ingredients except cream and pour over chicken. Cover and cook on Low setting for 8 to 10 hours (on High setting for 4 to 5 hours). Just before serving, stir in heavy cream. Serve over hot spaghetti.

6 to 8 servings (about 2½ quarts).

Cock 'n Bull Stew

¼ cup steak sauce	1 medium onion, chopped
2 chicken bouillon cubes	2 medium potatoes, peeled
1 teaspoon salt	and cubed
½ teaspoon pepper	2 medium carrots, pared
1 teaspoon sugar	and thinly sliced
½ cup hot water	1 can (16 oz.) stewed
2 to 3 lb. chicken parts,	tomatoes
preferably thighs	¼ cup flour
1 lb. lean stewing beef,	
cut into 1½-inch cubes	

Combine steak sauce, bouillon cubes, salt, pepper, sugar and hot water in Crock-Pot; stir well. Add remaining ingredients except flour; mix carefully. Cover and cook on Low setting for 8 to 10 hours (on High setting for 4 hours).

Before serving, remove chicken, bone and return meat to Crock-Pot; stir well. To thicken gravy, make a smooth paste of flour and ¼ cup juices from stew. Stir into Crock-Pot. Cover and cook on High setting until thickened.

6 to 8 servings (about 3½ quarts).

Chicken in Wine

3 lb. chicken parts,	1 can (4 oz.) sliced mush-
preferably breasts and	rooms, drained
thighs	½ cup dry sherry
Salt and pepper	1 teaspoon Italian
2 tablespoons butter	seasoning
1 medium onion, sliced	Fluffy rice

Rinse chicken parts and pat dry. Season chicken lightly with salt and pepper. In skillet, melt butter and quickly brown chicken parts; remove with slotted spoon and place in Crock-

Pot. Saute onion and mushrooms in skillet. Add sherry to skillet and stir, scraping to remove brown particles. Pour contents of skillet into Crock-Pot over chicken. Sprinkle with Italian seasoning. Cover and cook on Low setting for 8 to 10 hours (on High setting for 3 to 4 hours).

Serve chicken over fluffy rice and spoon sauce over top.

4 to 6 servings (about 2½ quarts).

Almond Chicken

---

1 can (14 oz.) chicken broth	1 small onion, sliced
1 slice bacon, diced	1 can (4 oz.) sliced mushrooms, drained
2 tablespoons butter	2 tablespoons soy sauce
¾ to 1 lb. boned chicken breasts, cut into 1-inch pieces	1 teaspoon monosodium glutamate
1½ cups diagonally sliced celery	Fluffy rice
	⅔ cup slivered almonds, toasted

Pour chicken broth into Crock-Pot. Cover and turn Crock-Pot to High setting while browning meats and vegetables.

In skillet, heat bacon and butter; add chicken pieces and brown quickly on all sides. With slotted spoon, remove browned chicken to Crock-Pot. Quickly sauté celery, onion and mushrooms in skillet until just slightly limp.

Add contents of skillet to Crock-Pot with soy sauce and monosodium glutamate; stir well. Cover and cook on Low setting for 6 to 8 hours (on High setting for 3 to 4 hours).

Serve over hot fluffy rice and garnish with toasted almonds.

4 servings (about 2 quarts).

Chicken Breasts à l'Orange

3 whole chicken breasts,
  halved
⅔ cup flour
1 teaspoon salt
1 teaspoon nutmeg
½ teaspoon cinnamon
  Dash pepper
  Dash garlic powder
2 to 3 sweet potatoes,
  peeled and cut into
  ¼-inch slices

1 can (10¾ oz.) condensed
  cream of celery or
  cream of chicken soup
1 can (4 oz.) sliced mushrooms, drained
½ cup orange juice
½ teaspoon grated orange
  rind
2 teaspoons brown sugar
3 tablespoons flour
  Buttered rice

Rinse chicken breasts and pat dry. Combine ⅔ cup flour with salt, nutmeg, cinnamon, pepper and garlic powder. Thoroughly coat chicken in flour mixture.

Place sweet potato slices in bottom of Crock-Pot. Place chicken breasts on top.

Combine soup with remaining ingredients except buttered rice; stir well. Pour soup mixture over chicken breasts. Cover and cook on Low setting for 8 to 10 hours (on High setting for 3 to 4 hours) or until chicken and vegetables are tender.

Serve chicken and sauce over hot buttered rice.

6 servings (about 3½ quarts).

A WAY WITH CHICKEN

Be sure to wash chicken well and pat dry—especially if you don't plan to pre-brown it. You might even try soaking it in lightly salted water in the refrigerator for 8 to 10 hours before using it in the Crock-Pot—some say the flavor is even better. If you like your chicken firm and dry, reduce the amount of liquid called for in the recipe.

Chicken Delicious

4 to 6 whole chicken breasts, boned and halved
Lemon juice
Salt and pepper
Celery salt
Paprika
1 can (10¾ oz.) condensed cream of mushroom soup
1 can (10¾ oz.) condensed cream of celery soup
⅓ cup dry sherry or white wine
Grated Parmesan cheese
Fluffy rice

Rinse chicken breasts and pat dry. Season with lemon juice, salt, pepper, celery salt and paprika. Place in Crock-Pot. In medium bowl or pan, mix mushroom and celery soups with sherry. Pour over chicken breasts. Sprinkle with Parmesan cheese. Cover and cook on Low setting for 8 to 10 hours.

Serve chicken and sauce over hot fluffy rice.

8 to 12 servings (about 3 quarts).

Baked Chicken Breasts

2 to 3 whole chicken breasts, halved
2 tablespoons butter or margarine
1 can (10¾ oz.) condensed cream of chicken soup
½ cup dry sherry
1 teaspoon leaf tarragon or leaf rosemary
1 teaspoon Worcestershire sauce
¼ teaspoon garlic powder
1 can (4 oz.) sliced mushrooms, drained

Rinse chicken breasts and pat dry; place in Crock-Pot. In saucepan, combine remaining ingredients and heat until smooth and hot. Pour over chicken breasts. Cover and cook on Low setting for 8 to 10 hours.

4 to 6 servings (about 2 quarts).

Chicken Curry

2 whole chicken breasts, boned
1 can (10¾ oz.) cream of chicken soup
¼ cup dry sherry
2 tablespoons butter or margarine

2 green onions with tops, finely chopped
1 teaspoon curry powder
1 teaspoon salt
Dash pepper
Fluffy rice or saffron rice

Cut chicken into small pieces; place in Crock-Pot. Add all remaining ingredients except rice. Cover and cook on High setting 2½ to 4 hours. Serve over hot rice.

4 servings (about 1½ quarts).

Double recipe for 5 quart Crock-Pot.

Hot Chicken Salad

2½ cups diced cooked chicken
1 cup toasted almonds
2 cups diagonally sliced celery
½ cup diced green pepper
3 tablespoons lemon juice
1 cup mayonnaise

3 tablespoons grated onion
1 cup cubed process cheese
1 cup crushed potato chips
½ cup grated Parmesan cheese
Toasted English muffins

Combine all ingredients in Crock-Pot except half the process cheese, half the potato chips, half the Parmesan cheese and the English muffins. Cover and cook on Low setting for 4 to 6 hours.

Just before serving, sprinkle with remaining process cheese, potato chips and Parmesan cheese. Serve on toasted English muffins.

6 to 8 servings (about 2 quarts).

Hot Turkey Salad: Substitute diced cooked turkey for the chicken.

Company Chicken Casserole

1 package (8 oz.) noodles	1½ cups cream-style cottage cheese
3 cups diced cooked chicken	1 cup grated sharp process cheese
½ cup diced celery	1 can (10¾ oz.) condensed cream of chicken soup
½ cup diced green pepper	
½ cup diced onion	
1 can (4 oz.) sliced mushrooms, drained	½ cup chicken broth
1 jar (4 oz.) pimiento, diced	2 tablespoons butter, melted
½ cup grated Parmesan cheese	½ teaspoon leaf basil

Cook noodles according to package directions in boiling water until barely tender; drain and rinse thoroughly. In large bowl, combine remaining ingredients with noodles, making certain the noodles are separated and coated with liquid. Pour mixture into greased Crock-Pot. Cover and cook on Low setting for 6 to 10 hours (on High setting for 3 to 4 hours).

6 servings (about 3 quarts).

Company Turkey Casserole: Substitute diced cooked turkey for the chicken.

Chicken Divan à la Crock-Pot

2 to 3 cups cooked cut-up
   chicken (large chunks)
½ small onion, chopped
1 can (10¾ oz.) condensed
   cream of chicken soup
½ cup mayonnaise
3 tablespoons flour
2 stalks celery, thinly sliced

1 package (10 oz.) frozen
   broccoli spears, thawed
   and cut into 1-inch
   pieces
½ teaspoon curry powder
1 tablespoon lemon juice
Hot buttered noodles

In medium bowl, thoroughly combine all ingredients except noodles. Pour into lightly greased Crock-Pot. Cover and cook on Low setting for 7 to 9 hours (on High setting for 2 to 3 hours).

Serve with hot buttered noodles, spooning sauce over top.

4 to 6 servings (about 2 quarts).

Turkey Divan à la Crock-Pot: Substitute cut-up cooked turkey for the chicken.

Chicken Spectacular

3 cups cut-up cooked
   chicken
1 can (16 oz.) cut green
   beans or peas, drained
2 cups cooked rice
1 can (10¾ oz.) condensed
   cream of celery soup
½ cup mayonnaise

1 can (6 or 8½ oz.) water
   chestnuts, drained
   and sliced
2 tablespoons chopped
   pimiento
2 tablespoons finely
   chopped onion

Combine all ingredients thoroughly. Pour into greased Crock-Pot. Cover and cook on Low setting for 6 to 8 hours.

4 servings (about 2 quarts).

FISH AND SEAFOOD

The proof that slow cooking and long cooking do not mean
overcooking shows up here like a whale in a lake.
Not claiming to be a broiler or sautéer, your Crock-Pot
concentrates on getting all the fish flavor there is to be had
from casseroles, chowders and stews. Many of these
recipes (and your own favorites, too) can be custom-tailored
to your personal likes. If you prefer chunky bits
in your chowders or casseroles, start the recipe
with half the amount of fish or seafood (for basic flavor);
then add the remainder an hour or two before serving.
And there's nothing wrong with using frozen fish either—
just stir to break it up after the first hour.

Fish 'n Vegetables

3 large flounder or red
  snapper fillets (about
  1 lb.), cut into 2-inch
  pieces
2 tablespoons olive oil or
  melted butter
1 clove garlic, minced
1 large onion, sliced
1 green pepper, seeded
  and cut into 1-inch
  pieces

1 to 2 zucchini (unpeeled),
  sliced
1 can (14½ oz.) whole
  tomatoes
½ teaspoon leaf basil
½ teaspoon leaf oregano
1 teaspoon salt
⅛ teaspoon pepper
¼ cup dry white wine

Combine all ingredients in Crock-Pot; stir thoroughly. Cover
and cook on High setting for 4 to 6 hours.

6 servings (about 3 quarts).

Halibut in Creamy Wine Sauce

2 packages (12 oz. each)
  frozen halibut steaks,
  thawed
2 tablespoons flour
1 tablespoon sugar
¼ teaspoon salt

¼ cup butter
⅓ cup dry white wine
⅔ cup milk or half-and-half
  cream
Lemon wedges

Pat halibut steaks dry; place in Crock-Pot. Combine flour, sugar
and salt.

In saucepan, melt butter; stir in flour mixture. When well
blended, add wine and milk and cook over medium heat
until thickened, stirring constantly. Allow sauce to boil 1
minute while stirring. Pour sauce over fish. Cover and cook on
High setting 2½ to 3 hours.

Transfer halibut to serving platter; garnish with lemon.

6 servings (about 2½ quarts).

Cioppino

1 lb. sea bass, cut into chunks	⅛ teaspoon seasoned pepper
1 can (4 oz.) sliced mushrooms, undrained	½ teaspoon leaf oregano
2 carrots, pared and sliced	1 can (7 oz.) clams, undrained
1 medium onion, chopped	½ lb. shelled, cleaned shrimp
1 small green pepper, seeded and chopped	1 small lobster tail (optional)
1 clove garlic, minced	1 package (6 oz.) frozen crabmeat, thawed and cartilage removed
1 can (15 oz.) tomato sauce	
1 can (14 oz.) beef broth	Minced parsley
Salt	

Combine half of sea bass in Crock-Pot with vegetables, garlic, tomato sauce, beef broth and seasonings; stir well. Cover and cook on Low setting for 10 to 12 hours (on High setting for 2 to 4 hours).

One hour before serving, turn to High setting and stir in remaining sea bass and seafood. Cover and cook on High setting for about 1 hour or until done.

Garnish with minced parsley and serve in soup plates. Accompany with hot Italian bread.

6 servings (about 3 quarts).

Fisherman's Catch Chowder

1- to 1½-lb. fish (use any
  combination of the
  following: flounder,
  ocean perch, pike,
  rainbow trout,
  haddock or halibut)
½ cup chopped onion
½ cup chopped celery
½ cup chopped pared carrots
¼ cup snipped parsley

¼ teaspoon leaf rosemary
1 can (16 oz.) whole
  tomatoes, mashed
½ cup dry white wine
1 bottle (8 oz.) clam juice
1 teaspoon salt
3 tablespoons flour
3 tablespoons butter or
  margarine, melted
⅓ cup light cream

Cut cleaned fish into 1-inch pieces. Combine all ingredients
except flour, butter and cream in Crock-Pot; stir well. Cover
and cook on Low setting for 7 to 8 hours (on High setting
for 3 to 4 hours).

One hour before serving, combine flour, butter and cream.
Stir into fish mixture. Continue to cook until mixture is
slightly thickened.

4 servings (about 2 quarts). Double recipe for 5-quart Crock-
Pot.

Chinese Cashew Tuna

1 can (7 oz.) tuna, drained
  and flaked
1 cup diced celery
½ cup minced onion
3 tablespoons margarine
1 can (10¾ oz.) condensed
  cream of mushroom
  soup

1 can (16 oz.) bean
  sprouts, drained
1 tablespoon soy sauce
1 cup cashew nuts,
  coarsely chopped
1 can (5½ oz.) chow mein
  noodles

Combine all ingredients except chow mein noodles in Crock-Pot; stir well. Cover and cook on Low setting for 5 to 9 hours (on High setting for 2 to 3 hours).

Serve over chow mein noodles.

4 servings (about 2 quarts).

Chinese Cashew Chicken: Substitute 1 cup diced cooked chicken for the tuna.

Tuna Salad Casserole

2 cans (7 oz. each) tuna,
  drained and flaked
1 can (10¾ oz.) condensed
  cream of celery soup
3 hard-cooked eggs,
  chopped

1½ cups diced celery
½ cup mayonnaise
¼ teaspoon pepper
1½ cups crushed potato
  chips

Combine all ingredients except ¼ cup of the crushed potato chips; stir well. Pour into greased Crock-Pot. Top with reserved potato chips. Cover and cook on Low setting for 5 to 8 hours.

4 servings (about 2 quarts).

Salmon and Potato Casserole

4 potatoes, peeled and
   thinly sliced
3 tablespoons flour
Salt and pepper
1 can (16 oz.) salmon,
   drained and flaked

1 medium onion, chopped
1 can (10¾ oz.) cream of
   mushroom soup
¼ cup water
Nutmeg

Place half of the potatoes in greased Crock-Pot. Sprinkle with half of the flour, salt and pepper. Cover with half the salmon; sprinkle with half the onion. Repeat layers in order.

    Combine soup and water. Pour over potato-salmon mixture. Dust with nutmeg. Cover and cook on Low setting for 7 to 10 hours.

6 servings (about 3 quarts).

Salmon-Wiches

1 can (16 oz.) salmon,
   drained and flaked
1 cup dry bread crumbs
2 eggs
¼ teaspoon leaf thyme
½ teaspoon celery salt

1 cup crushed cheese crackers
Vegetable oil
3 English muffins, split,
   toasted and buttered
2 cups Hollandaise sauce
Paprika

In bowl, combine salmon, bread crumbs, eggs, thyme and celery salt. Shape into 6 patties and coat well with crushed crackers. In skillet, saute patties in hot oil; drain. Transfer to Crock-Pot. Cover and cook on High setting for 2 to 3 hours. Place one patty on each English muffin half and top with Hollandaise. Sprinkle with paprika.

6 servings (about 1½ quarts).

Herbed Salmon Bake

2 chicken bouillon cubes
1 cup boiling water
1 can (16 oz.) salmon,
   drained and flaked
2 cups seasoned stuffing
   croutons

1 cup grated Cheddar
   cheese
2 eggs, beaten
¼ teaspoon dry mustard

Dissolve bouillon cubes in boiling water. Combine all ingredients; mix well. Pour into well-greased Crock-Pot. Cover and cook on High setting for 2 to 4 hours.

4 servings (about 1 ½ quarts).

Jambalaya

2 cups diced boiled ham
2 medium onions, coarsely
   chopped
2 stalks celery, sliced
½ green pepper, seeded
   and diced
1 can (28 oz.) whole
   tomatoes
¼ cup tomato paste
3 cloves garlic, minced

1 tablespoon minced
   parsley
½ teaspoon leaf thyme
2 whole cloves
2 tablespoons salad oil
1 cup raw long-grain
   converted rice
1 lb. fresh or frozen
   shrimp, shelled and
   cleaned

Thoroughly mix all ingredients except shrimp in Crock-Pot. Cover and cook on Low setting for 8 to 10 hours.

One hour before serving, turn Crock-Pot to High setting. Stir in uncooked shrimp. Cover and cook until shrimp are pink and tender.

4 to 6 servings (about 3 quarts).

Easy Shrimp Creole

2 tablespoons butter or
    margarine
⅓ cup chopped onion
2 tablespoons buttermilk
    biscuit mix
1½ cups water
1 can (6 oz.) tomato paste
1½ teaspoons salt
    Dash pepper
¼ teaspoon sugar

1 bay leaf
½ cup chopped celery
½ cup chopped green
    pepper
2 lb. frozen shrimp, thawed,
    shelled and cleaned,
    or 3 cans (5 oz. each)
    shrimp, rinsed and
    drained
Fluffy rice

In skillet, melt butter; add onion and cook slightly. Add biscuit mix and stir until well blended. Combine remaining ingredients except shrimp and rice and add with onion mixture to Crock-Pot; stir well. Cover and cook on Low setting for 7 to 9 hours.

One hour before serving, turn to High setting and add shrimp. Remove bay leaf and serve over hot fluffy rice.

6 *servings (about 1½ quarts)*. Double recipe for 5-quart Crock-Pot.

Shrimp Curry

3 chicken bouillon cubes
1 cup boiling water
1½ lb. shrimp, shelled and
    cleaned
2 cloves garlic, minced
1 teaspoon curry powder
½ teaspoon ground ginger

⅛ teaspoon nutmeg
    Dash cayenne pepper
½ cup milk
3 tablespoons flour
    Fluffy rice
    Curry accompaniments

Dissolve bouillon cubes in boiling water. Add with shrimp, garlic and spices to lightly oiled Crock-Pot; stir well. Cover and cook on High setting for 2 to 3 hours.

During last hour, make a smooth paste of milk and flour; stir into shrimp mixture. Cover and cook for 15 to 30 minutes or until thickened.

Adjust seasonings. Serve over rice with curry accompaniments: chutney, coconut, chopped green onions.

4 servings (about 1½ quarts). Double recipe for 5-quart Crock-Pot.

Sweet-and-Sour Shrimp

1 package (6 oz.) frozen Chinese pea pods, partially thawed	1 cup boiling water
	½ cup reserved pineapple juice
1 can (13 oz.) juice-pack pineapple chunks or tidbits (drain and reserve juice)	2 teaspoons soy sauce
	½ teaspoon ground ginger
	2 cans (4½ oz. each) shrimp, rinsed and drained
2 tablespoons cornstarch	
3 tablespoons sugar	2 tablespoons cider vinegar
1 chicken bouillon cube	Fluffy rice

Place pea pods and drained pineapple in Crock-Pot. In a small saucepan, stir together cornstarch and sugar. Dissolve bouillon cube in boiling water and add with juice, soy sauce and ginger to saucepan. Bring to a boil, stirring, and cook sauce for about 1 minute or until thickened and transparent. Gently blend sauce into pea pods and pineapple. Cover and cook on Low setting for 5 to 6 hours.

Before serving, add shrimp and vinegar, stirring carefully to avoid breaking up shrimp. Serve over hot rice.

4 to 5 servings (about 1½ quarts).

Seafood Normandy

2 lb. fresh or frozen
   shrimp, shelled and
   cleaned
1 tablespoon shrimp spice
   (in tea ball or tied in
   cheesecloth)
1 can (7½ oz.) Alaska king
   crabmeat, drained,
   flaked and cartilage
   removed
3 tablespoons tomato paste

½ teaspoon salt
1 teaspoon garlic salt
1 can (10¾ oz.) cream of
   shrimp soup
2 tablespoons water
2 teaspoons brandy or
   dry sherry
3 tablespoons milk
2 tablespoons flour
   Fluffy rice

Place all ingredients except milk, flour and rice in Crock-Pot; stir well. Cover and cook on High setting for 3 to 5 hours. Remove shrimp spice.

Before serving, make a smooth paste of milk and butter; stir into Crock-Pot. Cover and cook for 30 minutes or until thickened. Serve over fluffy rice.

4 to 6 servings (about 2½ quarts).

Swiss-Crab Casserole

3 tablespoons butter
½ cup chopped celery
½ cup chopped onion
¼ cup chopped green
    pepper (optional)
3 tablespoons flour
3 chicken bouillon cubes
2½ cups boiling water
1 cup quick-cooking
    rice
2 cans (7 oz. each) crab-
    meat, drained, flaked
    and cartilage removed

2 cups grated Swiss
    cheese
1 can (4 oz.) sliced mush-
    rooms, drained
¼ cup sliced pimiento-
    stuffed olives
¼ cup sliced almonds
    (optional)
1 cup buttered bread
    crumbs
½ cup grated Swiss cheese

In skillet, melt butter and lightly sauté celery, onion and green pepper. Remove from heat and blend in flour. Dissolve bouillon cubes in boiling water. Add to skillet and bring to a boil, stirring constantly. Cook sauce over medium heat for about 2 minutes or until slightly thickened.

Lightly toss remaining ingredients except buttered crumbs and ½ cup grated cheese in Crock-Pot. Add sauce; stir lightly to blend. Cover and cook on High setting for 3 to 5 hours.

Pour contents of Crock-Pot into shallow heatproof serving dish. Cover with buttered bread crumbs and sprinkle with ½ cup grated cheese. Set under broiler until cheese is melted and bread crumbs are crunchy brown.

4 to 6 servings (about 2 quarts).

Scalloped Oysters

2 cans (12 oz. each)
  frozen oysters and
  liquid, thawed
3½ cups coarsely crushed
  saltine crackers
⅔ cup grated Parmesan
  cheese
2 eggs, beaten
2 tablespoons dry sherry
½ cup butter, melted

Break up oysters into small pieces. Combine all ingredients, reserving 2 tablespoons of the melted butter; mix well. Pour into lightly greased Crock-Pot. Drizzle reserved butter over top. Cover and cook on Low setting for 7 to 9 hours (on High setting for 3 to 4½ hours).

4 servings (about 1½ quarts). Double recipe for 5-quart Crock-Pot.

Clam Casserole

3 cans (6½ oz. each)
  minced clams, drained
4 eggs, well beaten
¼ cup butter, melted
⅓ cup milk
1 teaspoon salt
½ cup minced onion
¼ cup minced green
  pepper
18 saltine crackers,
  coarsely crushed
  (about 1 cup)

In bowl, mix all ingredients. Pour into well-greased Crock-Pot. Cover and cook on Low setting for 5 to 6 hours.

6 servings (about 2½ quarts).

BEANS, RICE AND PASTA

The words "pot" and "beans" are such a natural twosome
that you might think the Crock-Pot was invented just because.
In fact, the results of these recipes are so sensational—and so
sensationally easy—you can't tell whether they started
with canned beans or the start-from-soak kind.
The Crock-Pot also works its slow-paced magic
on the bean's cousins—rice and pasta.
For best rice results, use long-grain converted rice in
recipes that cook for 8 hours or longer.
And any precooked pasta should be al dente (barely tender).
So, whether you're looking for a stylish side dish
or a change-of-pace entrée, these stick-to-the-ribs recipes
are sure to offer you plenty of choices.

Old-Fashioned Baked Beans

1 lb. dried pea (navy)
   beans
1 medium onion, finely
   chopped
½ cup ketchup
½ cup brown sugar
   (packed)

½ cup dark corn syrup
1 teaspoon paprika
½ teaspoon leaf basil
Salt
1 lb. smoked ham, bacon
   or salt pork, diced

Completely soften beans as directed below. Drain and stir in remaining ingredients. Pour into Crock-Pot. Cover and cook on Low setting for 6 to 12 hours (on High setting for 3 to 4 hours).

8 servings (about 2½ quarts).

A BIT ABOUT BEANS

Cooking with dried beans can be tricky, even in a Crock-Pot. The minerals in the water and variations in voltage affect different types of beans in different ways. For best results, keep these points in mind:

• Dried beans, especially red kidney beans, should be boiled before adding to a recipe. Cover the beans with 3 times their volume of unsalted water and bring to a boil. Boil 10 minutes, reduce heat, cover and allow to simmer 1½ hours or until beans are tender. Soaking in water, if desired, should be completed before boiling. Discard water after soaking or boiling.

• Sugar and acidic foods, such as tomatoes, tend to have a hardening effect on beans; therefore, always soften beans thoroughly before using them in baked beans, chili and similar recipes.

Saucy Baked Beans

3 cans (16 oz. each) baked
  beans in sauce, drained
1 medium onion, chopped
1 medium green pepper,
  seeded and chopped
½ cup brown sugar
  (packed)
2 tablespoons prepared
  mustard

1 teaspoon Worcestershire
  sauce
½ cup smoky barbecue
  sauce
Dash Tabasco sauce
2 tablespoons dried parsley
  flakes
4 to 6 slices cooked ham,
  diced

Combine all ingredients except ham in Crock-Pot; stir well. Sprinkle ham over top, pushing half down into beans. Cover and cook on Low setting for 5 to 12 hours (on High setting for 3 to 4 hours).

12 servings (about 3 quarts).

NOTE: If you want to cook beans the maximum time, do not completely drain liquid from canned beans.

Our Best Baked Beans

5 slices bacon, crisply
  fried and crumbled
2 cans (16 oz. each) baked
  beans, drained
½ green pepper, seeded
  and chopped
½ medium onion,
  chopped

1½ teaspoons prepared
  mustard
½ cup ketchup
½ cup hickory-smoke
  barbecue sauce
½ cup brown sugar
  (packed)

Mix all ingredients in Crock-Pot. Cover and cook on Low setting for 8 to 12 hours (on High setting for 3 to 4 hours).

6 to 8 servings (about 1½ quarts).

Beef 'n Beans

1 lb. dried pinto beans	2 cloves garlic, minced
¼ lb. salt pork or bacon, diced	1 can (6 oz.) tomato paste
1 to 2 lb. chuck steak, cut into 1-inch cubes	1 can (6 oz.) water
⅛ to ¼ teaspoon crushed red pepper	1 tablespoon chili powder
	Salt
	1 teaspoon ground cumin

Completely soften beans as directed on page 100. In skillet, brown salt pork and cubed chuck steak over medium-heat; drain well. Add to Crock-Pot with soaked pinto beans. Add remaining ingredients; stir well. Cover and cook on High setting for 2 hours, then on Low setting for 7 to 12 hours (or cook entire time on High setting for 5 to 8 hours).

8 servings (about 2½ quarts).

Bean Potpourri

2 cans (15 oz. each) garbanzos	3 slices bacon, crisply fried and crumbled
1 can (16 oz.) pinto beans, undrained	1 lb. cross-cut beef shank
4 medium potatoes, peeled and diced	½ lb. smoked ham hock
1 large onion, thinly sliced	3 to 4 oz. Polish sausage or knockwurst, thinly sliced
2 teaspoons salt	2½ cups water

Combine all ingredients in Crock-Pot; stir well. Cover and cook on Low setting for 8 to 16 hours (on High setting for 4 to 6 hours).

8 to 10 servings (about 3 quarts).

Burger 'n Bean Hot Dish

1 lb. ground beef
1 can (16 oz.) barbecue
   beans
1 can (11½ oz.) condensed
   bean with bacon soup
⅛ teaspoon seasoned black
   pepper

¼ teaspoon chili powder
½ teaspoon garlic salt
1 tablespoon instant
   minced onion
½ cup grated process
   American cheese

In skillet, brown ground beef; drain well. Thoroughly combine all ingredients except cheese in Crock-Pot. Cover and cook on Low setting for 6 to 9 hours.

Just before serving, sprinkle with grated cheese. Serve over hot corn bread.

6 servings (about 2 quarts).

Sausage Bean Quickie

4 to 6 cooked brown 'n
   serve sausage links,
   cut into 1-inch pieces
2 teaspoons cider vinegar
2 cans (16 oz. each) red
   kidney or baked beans,
   drained

1 can (7 oz.) pineapple
   chunks, undrained
2 teaspoons brown sugar
3 tablespoons flour

Combine sausage, vinegar, beans and pineapple in Crock-Pot. Mix brown sugar with flour and add; stir well. Cover and cook on Low setting for 7 to 10 hours (on High setting for 2 to 3 hours).

4 servings (about 1½ quarts).

Hearty Bean Stew

3 cans (15 oz. each) brown
    beans, drained
2 lb. extra-lean hamburger
2 cans (10¾ oz. each)
    condensed tomato soup

1 can (11 oz.) condensed
    Cheddar cheese soup
Salt and pepper

Combine all ingredients in Crock-Pot; stir well. Cover and cook on Low setting for 8 to 10 hours (on High setting for 3 to 4 hours).

8 to 10 servings (about 3 quarts).

Emergency Shelf Casserole

2 cans (28 oz. each) baked
    beans, partially drained
1 can (8 oz.) Vienna
    sausage links, drained
1 can (12 oz.) luncheon
    meat, cubed

¼ lb. dry salami, sliced
    (optional)
1 tablespoon minced onion
¼ teaspoon garlic powder
⅛ teaspoon leaf thyme

Combine all ingredients in Crock-Pot; stir well. Cover and cook on Low setting for 7 to 9 hours. Remove cover and cook on High setting to reduce excess liquid.

8 servings (about 3½ quarts).

KNOW YOUR BEANS

One type of dried bean may be substituted for any other type providing the measure is the same. Look over the bean soup recipes (pages 125–7) and tailor them to your own taste.

Barbecued Lamb'n Dried Limas

1 cup dried baby lima
    beans
2 lb. boneless lamb
    shoulder, well trimmed
    and cut into 1½-inch
    cubes
1 teaspoon salt

1 medium onion, chopped
1 small green pepper,
    seeded and chopped
1 can (8 oz.) tomato sauce
2 tablespoons brown sugar
1 tablespoon Worcester-
    shire sauce

Completely soften beans as directed on page 100. Combine all
ingredients in Crock-Pot; stir thoroughly to coat lima beans and
lamb. Cover and cook on Low setting for 10 to 12 hours.

4 servings (about 3 quarts).

Lamb Shanks with Split Peas

1 cup dried split green
    peas
3 lb. lamb shanks
1 large onion, chopped

2 carrots, pared and sliced
2 stalks celery, sliced
2½ cups beef broth
    Salt and pepper

Completely soften beans as directed on page 100. Brown lamb
shanks under broiler to remove fat; drain well. Mix all ingredients
except shanks in Crock-Pot; stir well. Add shanks, pushing down
into liquid. Cover and cook on Low setting for 10 to 12 hours.

4 to 6 servings (about 3 quarts).

Yellow Rice

2 cups raw long-grain
  converted rice
4½ cups water
¼ cup butter, melted

½ cup brown sugar
2½ teaspoons turmeric
2 teaspoons salt
½ to 1 cup raisins

Combine all ingredients in Crock-Pot; stir well. Cover and cook on Low setting for 8 to 9 hours (on High setting for 2 to 3 hours).

6 to 8 servings (about 2½ quarts).

Saffron Rice: Substitute ¾ teaspoon saffron threads for the turmeric and omit brown sugar and raisins.

Arroz con Queso

1½ cups raw long-grain
  converted rice
1 can (16 oz.) whole
  tomatoes, mashed
1 can (16 oz.) Mexican-
  style beans
3 cloves garlic, minced
1 large onion, finely
  chopped

2 tablespoons vegetable
  oil
1 cup cottage cheese
1 can (4 oz.) green chili
  peppers, drained,
  seeded and chopped
2 cups grated Monterey
  Jack or process
  cheese

Mix thoroughly all ingredients except 1 cup of the grated cheese. Pour mixture into well-greased Crock-Pot. Cover and cook on Low setting for 6 to 9 hours.

Just before serving, sprinkle with reserved grated cheese.

6 to 8 servings (about 2½ quarts).

Brown-and-White Rice

8 slices bacon, diced
½ cup raw brown rice
4 green onions with tops,
    sliced
1 can (4 oz.) sliced mush-
    rooms, drained
1 cup raw long-grain
    converted rice

3 cups beef broth
⅓ cup slivered almonds,
    toasted
3 tablespoons grated
    Parmesan cheese

In skillet, fry bacon until partially crisp but still limp. Stir in brown rice and cook over medium heat until rice is a light golden brown. Add bacon and browned rice to Crock-Pot with green onions, mushrooms, white rice and broth; stir well. Cover and cook on Low setting for 6 to 8 hours (on High setting for 2½ to 3½ hours). Before serving, stir well; add salt if needed. Garnish with almonds and cheese.

6 to 8 servings (about 2 quarts).

Golden Cheese Bake

2 cups cooked long-grain
    converted rice
3 cups pared and grated
    carrots
2 cups grated sharp
    process cheese

½ cup milk
2 eggs, beaten
2 tablespoons chopped
    onion
1½ teaspoons salt
¼ teaspoon pepper

In bowl, combine all ingredients; stir well. Pour into greased Crock-Pot. Cover and cook on Low setting for 7 to 9 hours (on High setting for 2½ to 3 hours).

4 to 6 servings (about 2 quarts). Double recipe for 5-quart Crock-Pot.

Wild Rice Casserole

½ cup butter or margarine, melted
3 stalks celery, thinly sliced
2 medium onions, finely chopped
1 can (10¾ oz.) condensed cream of mushroom soup

2½ cups water
2 packages (7 oz. each) wild rice and long-grain converted rice mix
1 can (4 oz.) sliced mushrooms, drained
½ lb. process American cheese, cubed

Combine all ingredients in Crock-Pot; stir thoroughly. Cover and cook on Low setting for 6 to 10 hours (on High setting for 2 to 3½ hours).

6 to 8 servings (2½ quarts).

Venetian Rice

2 cups diced cooked ham
1 slice bacon, diced
1 medium onion, finely chopped
2 stalks celery, thinly sliced
1 package (10 oz.) frozen peas, thawed

¾ cup raw long-grain converted rice
1½ cups chicken broth
Salt and pepper
Grated Parmesan cheese

Combine all ingredients except Parmesan cheese in Crock-Pot; stir well. Cover and cook on Low setting for 7 to 10 hours (on High setting for 3 to 4 hours).

Taste for seasoning. Just before serving, sprinkle top with Parmesan cheese.

6 servings (about 2 quarts).

Sausage-Rice Casserole

1 lb. bulk sausage	2 stalks celery, diced
1 envelope (1½ oz.) dry chicken soup mix	⅓ cup slivered almonds
¾ cup raw long-grain converted rice	4 cups water Salt

In skillet, brown sausage; drain well. Combine all ingredients in lightly greased Crock-Pot; stir well. Cover and cook on Low setting for 7 to 10 hours (on High setting for 3 to 4 hours or until rice is tender).

4 servings (about 1½ quarts).

Polenta/Cornmeal Mush

2 to 4 tablespoons butter or margarine, melted	2 cups cornmeal (preferably water ground)
¼ teaspoon paprika Dash cayenne pepper	2 teaspoons salt
6 cups boiling water	

Use 1 tablespoon butter to lightly grease walls of Crock-Pot. Add paprika and cayenne. Turn to High setting while measuring remaining ingredients. Add to Crock-Pot with remaining melted butter; stir well. Cover and cook on Low setting for 6 to 9 hours (on High setting for 2 to 3 hours, stirring occasionally).

8 to 10 servings (about 1½ quarts).

Fried Polenta or Cornmeal Mush: Pour hot cornmeal into 2 lightly greased loaf pans. Chill overnight. To serve, cut into ¾-inch slices and fry in butter until browned.

Cracked Wheat Pilaf

2 cups cracked wheat or
  bulgur
1 medium onion, chopped
5 cups beef broth
¼ cup butter, melted

¼ cup minced parsley or
  2 tablespoons dried
  parsley flakes
Salt

Combine all ingredients in Crock-Pot; stir well. Cover and cook on Low setting for 10 to 12 hours (on High setting for 3 to 4 hours, stirring occasionally).

6 to 8 servings (about 3 quarts).

Pennsylvania Dutch Scrapple

2 lb. pork neck bones
1 large onion, finely
  chopped

Salt and pepper
2½ cups cornmeal
Butter or margarine

Place neck bones, onion, salt and pepper in Crock-Pot; add enough water to cover. Cover and cook on Low setting for 7 to 12 hours.

With slotted spoon, take neck bones from broth. Remove meat from bones and return to broth in Crock-Pot. Stir in cornmeal. Cover and cook on Low setting for 6 to 10 hours (on High setting for 2 to 3 hours).

Taste for seasoning. Pour cornmeal mixture into 2 lightly oiled loaf pans. Chill overnight. Cut into ½-inch slices and fry.

12 to 15 servings (about 2 quarts).

Noodles Romanoff

1 package (8 oz.) noodles	4 green onions with tops,
2 tablespoons vegetable	finely minced
oil or melted butter	2 teaspoons Worcester-
1½ cups (12 oz.) sour cream	shire sauce
⅓ cup flour	Dash Tabasco sauce
1½ cups small-curd cream-	2 teaspoons garlic salt
style cottage cheese	

Cook noodles according to package directions until barely tender. Rinse in cold water and drain. Toss with oil. In large bowl, mix sour cream and flour. Stir in remaining ingredients. Add noodles and stir well to coat. Pour into well-greased Crock-Pot. Cover and cook on Low setting for 4 to 6 hours.

8 servings (about 2½ quarts).

Corned Beef and Noodles

1 package (8 oz.) noodles	¼ lb. process American
2 tablespoons vegetable	cheese, diced
oil	1 can (4 oz.) sliced mush-
1½ to 2 cups diced cooked	rooms, drained
corned beef	¾ cup milk
1 can (10¾ oz.) condensed	½ cup chopped onion
cream of chicken soup	Salt and pepper

Cook noodles according to package directions until barely tender; rinse in cold water and drain. In large bowl, toss with oil. Mix remaining ingredients with noodles. Pour into greased Crock-Pot. Cover and cook on Low setting for 8 to 9 hours (on High setting for 3 hours).

4 servings (about 2½ quarts).

Dried Beef 'n Noodles

3 to 4 oz. dried beef
1 package (8 oz.) noodles
2 teaspoons vegetable oil
¼ cup butter or margarine
¼ cup flour
2 cups evaporated milk

1 package (10 oz.) frozen
  peas or frozen mixed
  vegetables, partially
  thawed
1 package (8 oz.) sharp
  process cheese, grated

Snip dried beef into small pieces; set aside. Cook noodles according to package directions until barely tender. In large bowl, toss with oil; set aside. In saucepan, melt butter over medium heat. Blend in flour until smooth. Gradually stir in evaporated milk. Cook until smooth and thick.

Pour white sauce over noodles; toss to mix. Fold in snipped beef, vegetables and most of grated cheese, reserving a small amount to sprinkle over top; stir well. Pour mixture into well-greased Crock-Pot. Sprinkle lightly with reserved cheese. Cover and cook on Low setting for 6 to 10 hours.

4 to 6 servings (about 2½ quarts).

Macaroni and Cheese

3 cups cooked macaroni
1 tablespoon butter or
  margarine, melted
2 cups evaporated milk
3 cups shredded sharp
  process cheese

¼ cup finely chopped green
  pepper
¼ cup chopped onion
1 teaspoon salt
¼ teaspoon pepper

Toss macaroni with butter or margarine. Add remaining ingredients. Pour into lightly greased Crock-Pot. Cover and cook on High 2 to 3 hours, stirring once or twice.

Spaghetti with Meatballs

2 tablespoons olive oil or
  butter
1 clove garlic, minced
1 medium onion, finely
  chopped
1 can (28 oz.) Italian-style
  tomatoes, mashed
2 teaspoons salt
½ teaspoon sugar

1 teaspoon leaf basil
1 teaspoon leaf oregano
1 can (6 oz.) tomato paste
¼ teaspoon crushed red
  pepper
Meatballs (below)
2 packages (16 oz. each)
  spaghetti
Grated Parmesan cheese

Combine all ingredients except Meatballs, spaghetti and cheese in Crock-Pot; stir well. Cover and cook on Low setting for 5 to 10 hours. Add Meatballs and continue to cook on Low setting for 7 to 12 hours.

Just before serving, cook spaghetti according to package directions. Serve topped with Meatballs in sauce and pass grated Parmesan cheese.

10 to 12 servings (about 3½ quarts).

MEATBALLS

1 lb. lean ground beef
½ lb. lean ground pork
1 teaspoon garlic salt
¼ cup grated Parmesan
  cheese
⅛ teaspoon freshly ground
  pepper
½ teaspoon leaf basil

½ teaspoon leaf oregano
¼ teaspoon leaf thyme
¾ cup dry bread crumbs
⅓ cup pine nuts (optional)
2 tablespoons dried parsley
  flakes
2 eggs
¼ cup evaporated milk

Mix all ingredients thoroughly. Shape into 24 meatballs about 1½ inches in diameter. Place on baking sheet and bake in 450° oven for 15 to 20 minutes or brown meatballs in skillet; drain.

Macaroni and Beef

1½ lb. lean ground beef
2 cups uncooked
   macaroni
½ medium onion, chopped
1 can (4 oz.) sliced mushrooms, drained

1 can (16 oz.) whole-
   kernel corn, drained
2 cans (10¾ oz. each)
   condensed tomato
   soup
Salt and pepper

In skillet, brown ground beef; drain well. Put into Crock-Pot.
Cook macaroni according to package directions until barely
tender; drain well. Add macaroni and remaining ingredients
to Crock-Pot. Stir just enough to blend. Cover and cook on
Low setting for 7 to 9 hours (on High setting for 3 to 4 hours).

4 to 6 servings (about 1½ quarts).

Nothing is as soul-stirring and stomach-satisfying as a
hot, hearty soup on a cold, bleak day. And nothing—
despite some claims to the contrary—equals the homemade kind.
With its just-right simmer, the Crock-Pot brings out
the tantalizing aroma and all the wholesome goodness.
Simply put the ingredients together . . .
and leave them to their own delicious devices.
Whether you want an appetizer soup, a main-course soup
or a healthy soup for snacking, you're sure to find
the answer here. And don't overlook the special sampling
of saucery. The Crock-Pot offers any sauce
worthy of the name its most important ingredient: time.

Beef Stock

3 lb. beef soup bones
1 to 2 onions, chopped
1 to 2 carrots, pared and
    chopped
2 stalks celery, chopped

2 tablespoons dried parsley
    flakes
2 peppercorns
2 teaspoons salt

Place all ingredients in Crock-Pot. Add enough water to cover. Cover and cook on Low setting for 12 to 24 hours (on High setting for 4 to 6 hours). If cooked on High setting, the stock will be lighter in color and less concentrated. Strain and refrigerate. Keeps well 4 to 5 days, or may be frozen.

8 cups strained stock (about 3½ quarts).

Veal Stock: Substitute veal bones for the beef bones.

Chicken Stock

1 to 2 lb. chicken or turkey
    necks, gizzards, hearts
    and feet, if available
    (do not use liver)
2 peppercorns

2 teaspoons salt
1 small onion, chopped
2 stalks celery with tops,
    chopped

Place all ingredients in Crock-Pot. Add water to cover. Cover and cook on Low setting for 10 to 18 hours. Strain through dampened cheesecloth before using. This freezes well.

8 cups strained stock (about 3½ quarts).

To Clarify Beef or Chicken Stock: Remove bones and vegetables from Crock-Pot. Turn to High setting for 15 minutes. Stir in 2 egg whites and egg shells. Allow to heat for 15 minutes to 1 hour. Strain through dampened cheesecloth.

Old-Fashioned Onion Soup

3 lb. large onions, peeled and thinly sliced	6 to 8 slices French bread, cubed
½ cup butter, melted	4 to 5 cups chicken broth

Place sliced onions in Crock-Pot; pour in butter and mix to coat onions thoroughly. Stir in cubed bread. Add chicken broth to cover; stir well. Cover and cook on Low setting for 10 to 18 hours (on High setting for 4 to 5 hours, stirring occasionally). Stir well during last hour.

6 to 8 servings (about 3 quarts).

Cream of Mushroom Soup

3 cans (4 oz. each) sliced mushrooms, drained	Salt and pepper
1 tablespoon butter or margarine	2 tablespoons flour
3 cups chicken broth	1 cup sour cream
2 tablespoons chopped onion	1 cup half-and-half cream or milk

In skillet, sauté sliced mushrooms in butter; place in Crock-Pot. Add chicken broth, onion, salt and pepper; stir well. Cover and cook on Low setting for 6 to 10 hours (on High setting for 2½ to 3 hours).

About 30 minutes before serving, turn to High setting. Mix flour and sour cream; add to Crock-Pot with half-and-half cream. Cook until slightly thickened.

6 servings (about 2 quarts).

Cream of Leek Soup: Omit mushrooms; add 3 cups chopped leeks and 2 cups diced peeled potatoes.

Corn Chowder

6 slices bacon, diced	1 tablespoon sugar
½ cup chopped onion	1 teaspoon Worcestershire
2 cups diced peeled	sauce
potatoes	1 teaspoon seasoned salt
2 packages (10 oz. each)	¼ teaspoon pepper
frozen whole-kernel	1 cup water
corn, broken apart	
1 can (16 oz.) cream-style	
corn	

In skillet, fry bacon until crisp; remove and reserve. Add onion and potatoes to bacon drippings and sauté for about 5 minutes; drain well. Combine all ingredients in Crock-Pot; stir well. Cover and cook on Low setting for 6 to 7 hours.

4 servings (about 1½ quarts).

Cucumber-Chicken Soup

2 medium cucumbers,	1 soup can water
peeled	1 can (14 oz.) chicken
2 cans (10¾ oz. each)	broth
condensed cream of	½ small onion, minced
chicken soup	Salt and pepper

Cut 8 thin slices from one of the cucumbers and reserve for garnish; finely chop remaining cucumbers.

In Crock-Pot, dilute cream of chicken soup with 1 can water. Add chicken broth, chopped cucumbers and remaining ingredients; stir well. Cover and cook on Low setting for 6 to 10 hours (on High setting for 2 to 3 hours). Serve hot. Garnish with reserved cucumber slices.

4 servings (about 1½ quarts).

Flavor-Filled Tomato Soup

1 can (46 oz.) tomato juice
1 can (8 oz.) tomato sauce
3 beef bouillon cubes
½ cup boiling water
3 peppercorns
½ bay leaf

¼ teaspoon leaf basil
½ small onion, thinly sliced
3 tablespoons sugar
2 whole cloves
1 tablespoon chopped
   celery leaves

Stir all ingredients together in Crock-Pot. Cover and cook on Low setting for 5 to 10 hours. If thicker soup is desired, turn to High setting and remove lid for last hour of cooking. Strain before serving.

6 servings (about 1½ quarts).

Hearty Vegetable Soup

2 lb. cross-cut beef shanks
1 tablespoon salt
1½ teaspoons Worcester-
   shire sauce
   Dash pepper
2 teaspoons dried parsley
   flakes
1 medium onion, chopped
1 package (10 oz.) frozen
   cut green beans,
   thawed

1 cup chopped celery
1 cup sliced pared carrots
1 cup diced peeled potatoes
   or turnips
1 can (16 oz.) whole
   tomatoes

Combine all ingredients in Crock-Pot. Add water to cover barely (about 2 cups); stir well. Cover and cook on Low setting for 12 to 18 hours (on High setting for 5 to 7 hours).

Before serving, remove meat and bones; cut meat into bite-size pieces and stir into soup.

6 servings (about 3 quarts).

Italian Sausage Soup

1 to 1½ lb. sweet Italian
   link sausage, cut into
   1-inch pieces
2 cloves garlic, minced
2 medium onions, chopped
1 can (28 oz.) whole
   tomatoes, mashed
2 cans (14 oz. each) beef
   broth

1 teaspoon leaf basil
½ teaspoon leaf oregano
1 tablespoon chopped
   parsley
1 medium green pepper,
   seeded and chopped
2 zucchini, thinly sliced
1 to 2 cups water
Grated Parmesan cheese

In skillet, brown sausage; drain well. Add all ingredients except Parmesan cheese to Crock-Pot; stir well. Cover and cook on Low setting for 12 to 14 hours.

Taste for seasoning; serve sprinkled with cheese.

6 servings (about 3 quarts).

Minestrone Hamburger Soup

1 lb. lean ground beef
1 large onion, chopped
2 small potatoes, peeled
   and cubed
2 carrots, pared and sliced
2 stalks celery, sliced
1 can (28 oz.) whole
   tomatoes

1 cup shredded cabbage
1 small bay leaf
¼ teaspoon leaf thyme
¼ teaspoon leaf basil
1 teaspoon salt
¼ teaspoon pepper
Grated mozzarella or
   Parmesan cheese

Place all ingredients except cheese in Crock-Pot; stir thoroughly. Add water to cover. Cover and cook on Low setting for 8 to 12 hours (on High setting for 3 to 5 hours). Stir well. Serve sprinkled with cheese.

6 servings (about 3 quarts).

Hamburger and Sausage Soup

1 lb. lean ground beef
1 lb. Polish sausage, sliced
½ teaspoon seasoned salt
¼ teaspoon leaf oregano
¼ teaspoon leaf basil
1 envelope (1½ oz.) dry
   onion soup mix
6 cups boiling water
1 can (16 oz.) whole
   tomatoes

1 tablespoon soy sauce
1 cup sliced celery
¼ cup chopped celery
   leaves
1 cup sliced pared carrots
1 cup uncooked elbow
   macaroni
Grated Parmesan cheese

In skillet, brown ground beef and sausage; drain well. Place meat in Crock-Pot. Add seasonings, herbs and onion soup mix. Stir in boiling water, tomatoes and soy sauce. Add celery, celery leaves and carrots to meat mixture; stir well. Cover and cook on Low setting for 8 to 16 hours (on High setting for 4 to 5 hours).

One hour before serving, turn to High setting and stir in macaroni. Serve with Parmesan cheese.

4 to 6 servings (about 3½ quarts).

Scotch Broth

2 lb. lamb neck or breast,
    well trimmed
½ cup pearl barley
1 tablespoon salt
3 peppercorns
1 medium onion, chopped
2 stalks celery, sliced

1 medium turnip, peeled
    and diced
2 carrots, pared and sliced
1 package (10 oz.) frozen
    peas, thawed
1 teaspoon leaf thyme
¼ teaspoon Tabasco sauce

Combine all ingredients in Crock-Pot. Add water to cover; stir well. Cover and cook on Low setting for 10 to 12 hours (on High setting for 4 to 5 hours). Remove meat; bone and trim off any remaining fat. Dice meat. Skim off fat from liquid and return meat to Crock-Pot.

4 to 6 servings (about 3½ quarts).

Senegalese Cream Soup

2 medium onions, finely
    chopped
2 stalks celery, finely
    chopped
2 apples, peeled, cored
    and finely chopped
2 cans (14 oz. each)
    chicken broth

2 cups finely chopped
    cooked chicken
Dash cayenne pepper
Salt
2 tablespoons curry powder
¼ cup flour
¼ cup water
2 cups half-and-half cream

Combine onions, celery, apples, chicken broth, chicken, cayenne and salt in Crock-Pot. Mix curry powder with flour and water; stir into Crock-Pot. Cover and cook on Low setting for 6 to 7 hours.

One hour before serving, stir in half-and-half cream. Add additional thickening if needed. Serve hot or chilled.

4 to 6 servings (about 3 quarts).

Claudia's Brunswick Stew

2 to 3 cups ground cooked
   chicken
2 cups ground cooked pork
1 small onion, ground
2 cans (16 oz. each) whole
   tomatoes, mashed
2 cans (16 oz. each) cream-
   style corn

1 cup chicken broth
Salt and pepper
Dash Tabasco sauce
Dash Worcestershire
   sauce

Combine all ingredients in Crock-Pot; stir well. Cover and cook on Low setting for 6 to 9 hours (on High setting for 3 to 4 hours). Add more chicken broth after cooking, if desired. Season to taste before serving with additional salt, pepper, Tabasco and Worcestershire sauce. The longer the stew cooks, the better the flavor.

4 to 6 servings (about 2½ quarts).

Red Snapper Soup

1½ lb. red snapper fillets,
   cut into chunks
1 can (28 oz.) whole
   tomatoes, mashed
2 medium onions,
   chopped
1 package (10 oz.) frozen
   cut okra, thawed

½ cup minced shallots or
   green onions
2 tablespoons beef flavor
   base (paste or
   granules)
1 cup water
¼ cup dry sherry or water
Salt and pepper

Combine all ingredients in Crock-Pot; stir thoroughly. Cover and cook on High setting for 3 to 5 hours.

6 servings (about 3 quarts).

Crab Soup Carolina Style

2 cups white crabmeat,
    flaked and cartilage
    removed
1 can (10¾ oz.) cream of
    shrimp soup
3 tablespoons butter
2 strips (3 inches each)
    lemon peel

½ teaspoon ground mace
Salt and pepper
2 tablespoons dry sherry
    (optional)
2 cups milk

Combine all ingredients except milk in Crock-Pot; stir well. Cover and cook on Low setting for 3 to 5 hours. Stir in milk during last hour.

6 servings (about 2 quarts).

Shrimp Soup Carolina Style: Substitute 2 cups chopped shrimp for the crabmeat.

Super Simple Crab Bisque

1 package (10 oz.) frozen
    crabmeat, slightly
    thawed (retain liquid)
1 can (11 oz.) condensed
    tomato bisque or 1 can
    (10¾ oz.) condensed
    tomato soup

1 can (10¾ oz.) condensed
    cream of asparagus
    soup
1 cup half-and-half cream

Stir crabmeat and soups into lightly buttered Crock-Pot. Cover and cook on High setting for 3 to 4 hours, stirring occasionally. Stir in cream during last hour.

4 servings (about 1 quart).

Black Bean Soup

1 lb. black beans
3 cups water
¼ lb. bacon, fried crisp and
    crumbled, or ½ lb.
    smoked ham

2 medium onions, chopped
1 teaspoon garlic salt
¼ teaspoon coarsely ground
    pepper

Completely soften beans as directed on page 100. Combine all ingredients in Crock-Pot; stir well. Cover and cook on High setting for 4 to 6 hours.

8 servings (about 3 quarts).

Basil and Bean Soup

½ lb. dried white kidney
    beans or Great
    Northern beans
1 lb. lean stewing beef,
    cut into 1-inch cubes
2 small zucchini
    (unpeeled), diced
2 medium turnips, peeled
    and diced
1 large potato, peeled and
    diced

2 stalks celery, sliced
2 medium onions, chopped
1 can (28 oz.) whole
    tomatoes
2 teaspoons leaf basil
⅛ teaspoon crushed red
    pepper
1 tablespoon salt
2 tablespoons olive oil

Completely soften beans as directed on page 100. Combine all ingredients in Crock-Pot; add water to cover and mix well. Cover and cook on High setting for 3 hours, then turn to Low setting for 8 to 14 hours (or cook entire time on High setting for 5 to 7 hours).

6 servings (about 3½ quarts).

Lentil Soup

1 lb. dried lentils
2 smoked ham hocks
1 large onion, chopped
2 stalks celery, sliced

1 large carrot, pared and
   sliced
1 tablespoon sugar
¼ teaspoon leaf thyme

Completely soften beans as directed on page 100. Add remaining ingredients to Crock-Pot. Cover and cook on Low setting for 8 to 14 hours (on High setting for 4 to 6 hours).

8 servings (about 3½ quarts).

Cream of Lentil Soup

1 lb. dried lentils
1 medium onion, chopped
1 clove garlic, minced
1 medium carrot, pared
   and chopped

1 large stalk celery,
   chopped
3 cups water
1 cup heavy cream or half-
   and-half cream
Salt and pepper

Completely soften beans as directed on page 100. Add onion, garlic, carrot, celery and water to Crock-Pot. Cover and cook on Low setting for 8 to 10 hours (on High setting for 3 to 4 hours). Turn to Low setting and stir in cream; add salt and pepper to taste.

6 to 8 servings (about 2½ quarts).

Swedish Bean Soup

1 lb. dried pea (navy)
  beans
½ cup chopped onion
2 cups water

4 slices bacon, fried crisp
  and crumbled
Salt and pepper
1 cup milk

Completely soften beans as directed on page 100. Combine beans, 2 cups water and remaining ingredients except milk in Crock-Pot. Cover and cook on Low setting for 8 to 10 hours. Stir in milk during last hour.

6 to 8 servings (about 2½ quarts).

Fritz's Chili

1½ to 2 lb. ground chuck
1 package chili seasoning
  mix
1 large onion, chopped
3 cans (16 oz. each) chili
  beans with chili gravy
1 can (16 oz.) whole
  tomatoes, mashed

1 can (16 oz.) red kidney
  beans, drained
  (optional)
1 to 3 jalapeño peppers,
  finely chopped
  (optional)

In skillet, brown ground chuck; drain off fat. Add meat with remaining ingredients except jalapeño peppers to Crock-Pot; stir well. Cover and cook on Low setting for 8 to 10 hours (on High setting for 2½ to 4 hours). Before serving, stir in chopped peppers if hotter flavor is desired.

4 to 6 servings (about 3 quarts).

Male Chauvinist Chili

3 slices bacon, diced
½ lb. hot Italian link
  sausage, cut into
  1-inch pieces
½ lb. ground chuck
2 medium onions, chopped
1 small green pepper,
  seeded and chopped
2 cloves garlic, minced
1 jalapeño pepper, seeded
  and chopped
2 teaspoons Worcestershire
  sauce

1 to 3 teaspoons chili
  powder
½ teaspoon dry mustard
¼ teaspoon freshly ground
  pepper
2 cans (14 to 16 oz. each)
  Italian-style tomatoes
1 can (16 oz.) pinto beans,
  drained
1 can (16 oz.) garbanzos or
  kidney beans, drained

In large skillet, brown bacon pieces until crisp. Remove from skillet; drain well. Brown sausage and ground chuck with onions over medium heat; drain and add to Crock-Pot. Add bacon and remaining ingredients; stir well. Cover and cook on Low setting for 8 to 14 hours. Taste for seasoning.

6 to 8 servings (about 3½ quarts).

Fresh Tomato Sauce

4 cups peeled, seeded and finely chopped tomatoes	1½ teaspoons leaf basil
	1 teaspoon sugar
	1 can (6 oz.) tomato paste
1 medium onion, minced	3 cloves garlic, crushed

Combine all ingredients in lightly oiled Crock-Pot. Cover and cook on Low setting for 6 to 12 hours (on High setting for 4 hours). If a thicker sauce is desired, remove cover and cook on High setting until sauce is reduced.

This is good used in any recipe calling for tomato sauce.

About 5 cups. Double recipe for 5-quart Crock-Pot.

Super Taco Sauce

10 large tomatoes, peeled, or 2 cans (28 oz. each) whole tomatoes	1 tablespoon sugar
	1 tablespoon Worcestershire sauce
5 cloves garlic, chopped	2 to 3 jalapeño peppers, (optional)
2 teaspoons salt	
2 large onions, chopped	1 tablespoon flour
1 teaspoon chili powder	1 tablespoon vegetable oil
1 teaspoon leaf oregano	1 tablespoon wine vinegar
1 teaspoon leaf thyme	

Place all ingredients except flour, oil and vinegar in Crock-Pot; stir well. Cover and cook on Low setting for 8 to 10 hours. Remove cover and turn to High setting for last hour to reduce excess moisture.

Before removing sauce from Crock-Pot, stir in flour, oil and vinegar. Allow to cool. Pour 3 cups of sauce at a time into blender container; blend until smooth.

About 8 cups.

Meatless Spaghetti Sauce

1 eggplant (1 lb.), peeled
and cut into 1-inch
cubes
1 medium onion, chopped
2 cloves garlic, minced
1 teaspoon dried parsley
flakes
1 can (16 oz.) Italian-style
tomatoes

1 can (6 oz.) tomato paste
1 can (4 oz.) mushrooms,
undrained
1 teaspoon leaf oregano
1½ teaspoons salt
1 teaspoon sugar

Combine all ingredients in Crock-Pot; stir well. Cover and cook on Low setting for 10 to 12 hours (on High setting for 2 to 4 hours).

About 6 cups.

Spaghetti Meat Sauce

½ lb. sweet or hot Italian
link sausage
1 lb. ground chuck
1 lb. round steak or
stewing beef, cut into
1-inch cubes
2 medium onions, chopped
1 large green pepper,
seeded and chopped
2 cloves garlic, minced

2 tablespoons sugar
1 tablespoon salt
2 teaspoons leaf basil
⅛ teaspoon crushed red
pepper
2 cans (16 oz. each)
Italian-style tomatoes,
broken up
1 can (8 oz.) tomato sauce
1 can (6 oz.) tomato paste

Remove sausage from casings; brown in skillet with ground chuck and cubed meat. Break up sausage and ground meat with wooden spoon or fork as they brown; drain well. Add to Crock-Pot with remaining ingredients; stir well. Cover and cook on Low setting for 8 to 16 hours (on High setting for

4 to 6 hours). For thicker sauce, cook on High setting for last 2 hours, removing cover for last hour.

About 3½ quarts.

NOTE: This sauce may be made 1 to 2 days in advance and refrigerated. It also freezes well.

Marinara Sauce

2 cans (28 oz. each) whole tomatoes	1 clove garlic, chopped
1 onion, finely chopped	2 tablespoons vegetable oil
2 carrots, pared and finely chopped	1½ teaspoons sugar
	1½ teaspoons salt

Place tomatoes in batches in blender container; blend until smooth (or puree tomatoes through a food mill).

In skillet, sauté onion, carrots and garlic in oil just until tender (do not brown). Combine all ingredients in Crock-Pot; stir well. Cover and cook on Low setting for 6 to 10 hours. Remove cover, stir well and cook on High setting for the last hour for a thicker marinara sauce.

About 6 cups.

A SAUCE WHENEVER YOU NEED IT

All of the sauces on these pages can be made in advance and then frozen. Freeze in handy serving-size containers—you'll have just the right amount, just when you need it.

Chicken-Mushroom Pasta Sauce

2- to 3-lb. fryer, whole or
    cut up
2 stalks celery, sliced
2 onions, chopped
2 teaspoons salt
½ cup chicken broth or
    water
1 can (6 oz.) tomato paste
¼ cup dry sherry

1 teaspoon leaf oregano
1 lb. mushrooms, sliced,
    or 2 cans (4 oz. each)
    sliced mushrooms,
    drained
2 tablespoons butter
2 tablespoons flour
½ cup heavy cream or half-
    and-half cream

Place fryer in Crock-Pot with celery, onions and salt. Combine chicken broth with tomato paste and pour over ingredients in Crock-Pot. Add sherry, oregano and mushrooms; stir to moisten all ingredients. Cover and cook on Low setting for 8 to 10 hours (on High setting for 3½ to 5 hours).

Remove chicken; bone meat and dice. Return meat to Crock-Pot. Knead butter and flour together and add with cream; stir well. Cover and cook on High setting for 30 minutes to 1½ hours (on Low setting for 3 to 5 hours).

4 to 6 servings (about 3 quarts).

FOR CAREFREE CASSEROLES

Slow-cooking is ideal for casseroles. It gives the different ingredients plenty of time to mingle and meld, creating a mellower blend of flavors. Best of all, most casseroles can be put together the night before and refrigerated in a bowl or in the accessory Bread 'n Cake Bake pan. The following morning, simply pour the contents into a lightly greased Crock-Pot (or place the bake pan directly in the Crock-Pot); cover and cook the recommended time.

VEGETABLES

For a foodstuff so seemingly simple, vegetables are
as ornery as can be. They can lose color, vitamins, taste and
texture faster than you can say "Brussels sprouts."
And timing them to be ready with the rest of the menu
is often no mean feat. Crock-Pot to the rescue!
Vegetables retain their consistency, flavor, eye appeal and
nutritional value. As for timing? They're ready whenever you are.
(No more worries about a charred steak or a collapsed soufflé.)
Just look over the vegetables in variety
on the following pages. Temptingly sauced and cleverly seasoned,
they're sure to increase the membership of
the vegetable fan-club at your house.

Asparagus Casserole

2 packages (10 oz. each)
frozen asparagus
spears, thawed
1 can (10¾ oz.) condensed
cream of celery soup
1 can (10¾ oz.) condensed
cream of chicken soup

2 cups crushed saltine
crackers
1 cup cubed process
American cheese
1 egg
½ cup slivered almonds

In large bowl, combine all ingredients well. Pour into lightly greased Crock-Pot. Cover and cook on High setting for 3 to 3½ hours.

After cooking, dish may be held on Low setting for up to 2 hours before serving.

4 to 6 servings (about 2 quarts).

NOTE: Two cans (14½ oz. each) asparagus pieces, drained, may be substituted for frozen asparagus.

Sweet-and-Sour Green Beans

2 packages (10 oz. each)
frozen French-style
green beans, partially
thawed
4 slices bacon, diced
1 small onion, diced
1 tablespoon flour

¼ cup water
¼ cup cider vinegar
2 tablespoons sugar
½ teaspoon salt
Dash pepper
1 tablespoon chopped
pimiento

Break apart green beans and place in Crock-Pot. In skillet, fry bacon until crisp; remove bacon to absorbent towels to drain. Pour off all but 2 tablespoons bacon drippings from skillet; sauté onion in bacon drippings (do not brown). Dissolve flour in water; stir into bacon drippings and cook until slightly thickened. Combine bacon and remaining ingredients and stir into thickened onion mixture. Pour over green beans and stir well. Cover and cook on High setting for 1 hour, then turn to Low setting for 7 to 9 hours.

6 to 8 servings (about 2 quarts).

Lima Bean Casserole

2 small onions, thinly sliced
3 packages (10 oz. each) frozen baby lima beans, thawed
2 cans (10¾ oz. each) condensed cream of celery soup
2 cans (4 oz. each) sliced mushrooms, undrained

1 jar (2 oz.) chopped pimiento, drained
2 teaspoons salt
⅛ teaspoon pepper
½ teaspoon dill seed
½ cup heavy cream
1 cup grated Parmesan cheese

Combine all ingredients except heavy cream and Parmesan cheese in Crock-Pot; stir well. Cover and cook on Low setting for 10 to 12 hours. Just before serving, add cream and stir well; sprinkle Parmesan cheese on top.

8 to 10 servings (about 3 quarts).

Harvard Beets

½ cup sugar
2 tablespoons flour
¼ cup water

¼ cup white vinegar
2 cans (16 oz. each) whole
beets, drained

Mix sugar and flour; stir in water and vinegar. Place beets in Crock-Pot. Pour sugar-vinegar mixture over beets and stir to coat well. Cover and cook on High setting for 3 to 4 hours.

4 to 6 servings (about 1½ quarts).

Louise's Broccoli Casserole

2 packages (10 oz. each)
frozen broccoli
spears, thawed and
cut up
1 can (10¾ oz.) condensed
cream of celery soup

1¼ cups grated sharp
Cheddar cheese
¼ cup minced green onion
1 cup crushed saltine
crackers or potato
chips

In large bowl, combine broccoli, celery soup, 1 cup of the grated cheese and the minced onion. Pour into lightly greased Crock-Pot. Sprinkle top with crushed crackers, then with remaining cheese. Cover and cook on Low setting for 5 to 6 hours (on High setting for 2½ to 3 hours).

4 to 6 servings (about 2 quarts).

NOTE: If desired, casserole may be spooned into a baking dish and garnished with additional grated cheese and broken potato chips; bake for 5 to 10 minutes in a 400° oven.

Carrots Lyonnaise

1 chicken bouillon cube	¼ teaspoon salt
1 cup boiling water	6 carrots, pared and cut
2 onions, sliced	into julienne strips
¼ cup butter or margarine	1 to 2 tablespoons sugar
1 tablespoon flour	(optional)

Dissolve bouillon cube in boiling water; set aside. In large skillet, sauté onions in butter, stirring to separate rings and prevent browning. Stir flour and salt into slightly cooled bouillon; add to onions and cook until thickened. Combine carrots and onion sauce in Crock-Pot, stirring to coat carrots. Cover and cook on High setting for 1 hour, then turn to Low setting for 2 to 6 hours. Before serving, add sugar to taste.

6 to 8 servings (about 2 quarts).

Golden Cauliflower

2 packages (10 oz. each) frozen cauliflower, thawed	1 can (11 oz.) condensed Cheddar cheese soup
Salt and pepper	4 slices bacon, crisply fried and crumbled

Place cauliflower in Crock-Pot. Season with salt and pepper. Spoon Cheddar cheese soup over top; sprinkle with bacon. Cover and cook on High setting for 1½ hours, then turn to Low setting for 2 hours (or cook on Low setting only for 4 to 5 hours).

4 to 6 servings (about 2 quarts).

Golden Broccoli: Substitute frozen broccoli for the frozen cauliflower.

Braised Celery

1 bunch celery or 3 bunches
   celery hearts
1 cup beef broth
1 onion, finely chopped
1 carrot, pared and finely
   chopped

1 teaspoon tomato paste
   or ketchup
2 slices bacon, diced

Cut celery stalks diagonally into 1-inch pieces (about 4 to 5 cups). Put into Crock-Pot with remaining ingredients; stir well. Cover and cook on High setting for 2½ to 3½ hours (on Low setting for 8 to 10 hours).

6 to 8 servings (about 2 quarts).

Corn Pudding

4 eggs
1 can (17 oz.) cream-style
   corn
⅓ cup flour
1 teaspoon sugar
½ teaspoon salt

⅛ teaspoon pepper
½ cup half-and-half cream
   or milk
½ tablespoon butter, cut
   into bits

In large bowl; beat eggs until thick and lemon colored. Stir in corn. In another bowl, beat dry ingredients with half-and-half until smooth; stir into corn. Pour into greased Crock-Pot. Dot with butter. Cover and cook on High setting for 3 to 4 hours (on Low setting for 7 to 9 hours).

6 to 8 servings (about 1½ quarts).

Scalloped Eggplant

1 large eggplant, peeled
and diced
1 small onion, minced
1½ cups crushed saltine
crackers
2 teaspoons baking
powder

2 tablespoons butter or
margarine, melted
2 eggs
Evaporated milk to moisten
Salt and pepper
Grated process American
cheese (optional)

In saucepan, cook eggplant in enough boiling water to cover until tender, about 7 to 9 minutes; drain well. Mix eggplant with remaining ingredients except grated cheese. Pour into greased Crock-Pot. Sprinkle with grated cheese. Cover and cook on Low setting for 4 to 8 hours (on High setting for 1½ to 2 hours).

4 to 6 servings (about 2 quarts).

Pizza Potatoes

6 medium potatoes, peeled
and thinly sliced
1 large onion, thinly sliced
Olive oil
½ lb. grated mozzarella
cheese

2 oz. sliced pepperoni
1 teaspoon salt
1 can (8 oz.) pizza sauce

In skillet, sauté potato and onion slices in oil until onion begins to appear transparent; stir constantly to prevent browning. Drain well. Combine potatoes and onions with cheese, pepperoni and salt in Crock-Pot. Pour pizza sauce over top. Cover and cook on Low setting for 6 to 10 hours.

4 to 6 servings (about 2 quarts).

Potatoes Perfect

¼ lb. bacon, diced
2 medium onions, thinly
  sliced
4 medium potatoes, thinly
  sliced

½ lb. Gruyère or Cheddar
  cheese, thinly sliced
Salt and pepper
Butter

Line Crock-Pot with aluminum foil, leaving enough to overlap potatoes when finished. Layer half each of the bacon, onions, potatoes and cheese in Crock-Pot. Season to taste and dot with butter. Repeat layers of bacon, onions, potatoes and cheese. Dot with butter. Overlap with remaining foil. Cover and cook on Low setting for 10 to 12 hours (on High setting for 3 to 4 hours).

4 to 6 servings (about 3½ quarts).

Sweet Potato Casserole

2 cans (16 oz. each) sweet
  potatoes or yams,
  drained and mashed
½ cup milk
¼ cup dry sherry
6 tablespoons butter or
  margarine, softened

1 teaspoon freshly grated
  lemon peel
½ teaspoon salt
¼ teaspoon nutmeg
  Dash cayenne pepper
4 eggs

In a bowl, beat sweet potatoes, milk, sherry and butter with an electric mixer until smooth. Add remaining ingredients and beat well. Pour into greased Crock-Pot. Cover and cook on High setting for 1 hour, then turn to Low setting for 3 to 4 hours.

4 to 6 servings (about 2 quarts).

Squash Casserole

2 lb. yellow summer
squash or zucchini,
thinly sliced (about
6 cups)
½ medium onion, chopped
1 cup pared shredded
carrot
1 can (10¾ oz.) condensed
cream of chicken soup

1 cup sour cream
¼ cup flour
1 package (8 oz.) seasoned
stuffing crumbs
½ cup butter or margarine,
melted

In large bowl, combine squash, onion, carrot and soup. Mix sour cream and flour; stir into vegetables. Toss stuffing crumbs with butter and place half in Crock-Pot. Add vegetable mixture and top with remaining stuffing crumbs. Cover and cook on Low setting for 6 to 8 hours.

4 to 6 servings (about 2½ quarts).

Turnip Custard

2 lb. (about 4) turnips, peeled and diced	⅔ cup evaporated milk
1 egg, well beaten	1 teaspoon salt
¼ cup crushed saltine crackers	Dash pepper
	1 cup grated Cheddar cheese
	⅛ teaspoon allspice

In uncovered saucepan, cook turnips in boiling water until tender; drain well. Mash if necessary and drain. Blend in remaining ingredients. Pour into buttered Crock-Pot. Cover and cook on High setting for 2 to 3 hours (on Low setting for 4 to 6 hours).

4 to 6 servings (about 1½ quarts).

Zucchini Italiano

6 to 8 small zucchini (unpeeled), cut into ¼-inch slices	2 teaspoons leaf basil
1 small onion, thinly sliced and separated into rings	2 tablespoons dried parsley flakes
3 tablespoons olive oil	Dash freshly ground pepper
2 cloves garlic, minced	½ cup grated Parmesan cheese
1 to 2 teaspoons salt	2 ripe tomatoes, peeled and quartered

Combine all ingredients except Parmesan cheese and tomatoes in Crock-Pot; stir together thoroughly. Cover and cook on Low setting for 7 to 10 hours.

Before serving, pour into ovenproof casserole. Taste for seasoning. Sprinkle with Parmesan cheese and garnish with tomato quarters. Broil until cheese is lightly browned.

6 to 8 servings (about 2 quarts).

CROCK-POT SPECIALTIES

Now and then it makes great sense to let your Crock-Pot
do a little specialty work. All it calls for
is a "different" kind of thinking about your slow cooker.
And here are five delightfully different directions
to think about and explore:
Party Starters. . .for dips and snacks and hearth-warming drinks;
Dieter's Fare. . .for the growing army of calorie counters;
Gamesmanship. . .for tender treatment of the hunter's prize;
for the Twosome. . .right-size servings for the small family;
Group Gatherings. . .festive fare for the 6-quart size.
Talk about versatility—
you might think your Crock-Pot invented the word.

PARTY STARTERS

How about being a guest at your next party?
Start a dip, a meaty tidbit or a welcoming punch
well in advance of the company hour. Let your Crock-Pot
do the cooking while you do something else.
Then let the Crock-Pot do the serving while you tend
to merry mingling. With help like this, you may
end up being your own best guest.

Hot Crab Dip

3 packages (8 oz. each)
    cream cheese, cut up
    and softened
¼ to ½ cup milk
2 cans (6½ oz. each)
    crabmeat, drained,
    flaked and cartilage
    removed

½ cup chopped green
    onions with tops
1 teaspoon prepared
    horseradish
2 teaspoons Worcestershire
    sauce

Combine all ingredients in lightly greased Crock-Pot. Cover and cook on High setting until cheese begins to melt (about 30 minutes), stirring well occasionally.

Cover and continue to cook on High setting until mixture is smooth and cheese is melted. Add more milk if needed for dipping consistency; then turn to Low setting for 3 to 4 hours. Just before serving, remove cover. Serve as a hot dip with Melba toast rounds.

About 1 quart.

Clam Dip: Substitute 2 cans (7 oz. each) minced clams for crabmeat; use clam juice instead of milk to dilute mixture.

Mariners' Fondue

2 cans (10¾ oz. each)
  condensed cream of
  celery soup
2 cups grated sharp process
  cheese
1 cup chunked cooked
  lobster
½ cup chopped cooked
  shrimp
½ cup chopped cooked
  crabmeat
¼ cup finely chopped
  cooked scallops
Dash paprika
Dash cayenne pepper
1 loaf French bread,
  cut into 1-inch cubes

Combine all ingredients except bread cubes in lightly greased Crock-Pot; stir thoroughly. Cover and cook on High setting for 1 hour or until cheese is melted. Turn to Low for serving. Using fondue forks, dip bread cubes into fondue.

About 1½ quarts.

Hot Refried Bean Dip

1 can (16 oz.) refried beans,
  drained and mashed
½ lb. lean ground beef
3 tablespoons bacon fat
1 lb. process American
  cheese, cubed
1 to 3 tablespoons taco
  sauce
1 tablespoon taco spice
Garlic salt

In skillet, brown beans and ground beef well in bacon fat. Add to Crock-Pot. Stir in remaining ingredients. Cover and cook on High setting until cheese is melted, about 1 to 2 hours, stirring occasionally. Turn to Low setting until ready to serve, up to 6 hours. Serve with warm tortilla chips.

About 1½ quarts.

Hot Chili con Queso Dip

1½ cups half-and-half cream, scalded	¼ cup flour
½ lb. Monterey Jack cheese, grated	¼ cup water
½ lb. sharp process cheese, grated	1 can (4 oz.) green chili peppers, drained, seeded and chopped
1 tablespoon butter	1 to 2 tablespoons chopped jalapeño chili peppers (optional)
½ medium onion, minced	
1 medium clove garlic, minced	Salt and pepper
¼ cup dry white wine	Dash cayenne pepper

Pour scalded cream into buttered Crock-Pot. Turn to High setting and stir in grated cheeses.

In small skillet or saucepan, melt butter and sauté onion and garlic until onion is tender. Add wine and stir well. Add to cheese mixture in Crock-Pot. Combine the flour and water and stir in with remaining ingredients. Cover and cook on High setting for about 30 minutes or until cheese begins to melt. Turn to Low setting and stir about 2 or 3 times during first hour until smooth. Allow to cook on Low setting for 3 to 5 hours, stirring occasionally.

One hour before serving, remove cover. Add an additional 2 tablespoons flour and 2 tablespoons water if dip becomes too thin. Serve with tortilla chips and celery.

About 7 cups.

TOO MUCH DIP?

Freeze the leftovers for your next gathering. Cool the dip, pour into a freezer container and seal tightly (it will keep up to 2 months). To serve, thaw and heat in a saucepan.

Boiled Peanuts

1½ quarts green uncooked   ½ cup salt
    peanuts   2½ quarts water

Wash peanuts until water runs clear. Put clean peanuts in Crock-Pot. Add salt and water; stir well. Cover and cook on High setting for 5 to 7 hours. Add additional water during cooking to keep peanuts covered.

For a saltier flavor, turn Crock-Pot off and allow peanuts to stand overnight in cooking liquid.

Classic Swiss Fondue

1 clove garlic   3 tablespoons kirsch
2½ cups dry white Rhine,   Freshly ground
    Chablis or Riesling   nutmeg
    wine   Pepper
1 tablespoon lemon juice   Paprika
1 lb. Swiss cheese, grated   1 loaf Italian or French
½ lb. Cheddar cheese,   bread, cut into 1-inch
    grated   cubes
3 tablespoons flour

Rub an enameled or stainless steel pan with garlic clove. Heat wine to a slow simmer (just under boiling). Add lemon juice. Combine cheeses and flour and gradually stir in. Using a figure-8 motion, stir constantly until cheese is melted. Pour into lightly greased Crock-Pot. Add kirsch; stir well. Sprinkle with nutmeg, pepper and paprika. Cover and cook on High setting for 30 minutes, then turn to Low setting for 2 to 5 hours. Keep on Low setting while serving. Using fondue forks, dip bread cubes into fondue.

About 2 quarts.

Hot Broccoli-Cheese Dip

¼ cup butter
3 stalks celery, thinly
   sliced
1 medium onion, chopped
1 can (4 oz.) sliced
   mushrooms, drained
3 tablespoons flour
1 can (10¾ oz.) condensed
   cream of celery soup

1 garlic cheese roll (5 to
   6 oz.), cut up
1 package (10 oz.) frozen
   broccoli spears or
   chopped broccoli,
   thawed

In small skillet, melt butter and sauté celery, onion and mushrooms. Stir in flour. Turn into lightly greased Crock-Pot; stir in remaining ingredients. Cover and cook on High setting, stirring about every 15 minutes, until cheese is melted. Turn to Low setting for about 2 to 4 hours or until ready to serve. Serve hot with corn chips, raw cauliflowerets, carrot strips, celery chunks and radishes.

About 1 quart.

Shrimp in Beer

2 to 3 lb. shrimp in shells
2 cups beer
2 teaspoons salt

1 tablespoon mixed
   pickling spice

Wash shrimp in cold water; drain. Place in Crock-Pot. Add remaining ingredients; stir well. Cover and cook on High setting for 2 hours or until shrimp turn pink. If desired, turn to Low setting until serving time, up to 2 hours.

4 to 6 servings (about 2½ quarts).

Sausage Cocktail Balls

1½ lb. extra-lean bulk pork sausage	2 eggs
1 can (7 oz.) water chestnuts, drained and finely chopped	¾ cup dry bread crumbs
	½ teaspoon leaf basil
	Sauce (below)

Thoroughly combine all ingredients except Sauce; mix well. Shape into bite-size meatballs. Place on rack of broiler pan. Bake in preheated 425° oven for about 15 minutes; drain well.

Place browned sausage balls in lightly greased Crock-Pot. Cover and cook on Low setting for 5 to 6 hours. Serve on wooden picks for dipping into Sauce.

About 30 small meatballs (about 2 quarts).

SAUCE

¼ cup butter or margarine	2 to 3 teaspoons prepared mustard
¼ cup flour	¼ teaspoon dill weed
1½ cups milk	1 cup sour cream
Salt and pepper	

In saucepan, melt butter over medium heat. Blend in flour until smooth. Gradually stir in milk. Add remaining ingredients. Cook and stir until smooth and thick.

CROCK-POT CRISPING

Use your Crock-Pot to revive stale potato chips and crackers. Place them in the pot but do not cover. Heat on Low setting for 2 to 4 hours. Voila! They're crisp, warm and ready.

Barbecue Meatballs

1½ cups chili sauce
1 cup grape or currant
    jelly
1 to 3 teaspoons Dijon
    mustard

1 lb. lean ground beef
1 egg
3 tablespoons fine dry
    bread crumbs
½ teaspoon salt

Combine chili sauce, grape jelly and mustard in Crock-Pot; stir well. Cover and cook on High setting while preparing meatballs.

Combine remaining ingredients thoroughly. Shape into 30 small meatballs. Place on broiler rack or in baking pan. Bake in preheated 400° oven for 15 to 20 minutes; drain well. Add meatballs to sauce in Crock-Pot. Stir well to coat; cover and cook on Low setting for 6 to 10 hours. The longer the cooking, the more barbecue flavor absorbed.

Serve on wooden picks for appetizers. To serve as a main dish, shape meat mixture into larger meatballs and cook as directed.

30 small meatballs (about 2 quarts).

Polish Sausage in Beer

Fill Crock-Pot with Polish sausage, cut into 4-inch pieces. Add 1 can (12 oz.) beer. Cover and cook on Low setting for 5 to 8 hours (on High setting for 1½ to 2 hours).

Skewer sausage pieces and place on charcoal broiler to smoke and brown—about 5 minutes.

NOTE: Use bratwurst or kosher frankfurters instead of Polish sausage, if desired.

Bratwurst in Sauce

2 to 3 lb. uncooked bratwurst sausages	1 can (12 oz.) beer
1 can (6 oz.) tomato paste	½ small onion, finely chopped
½ cup ketchup	2 cloves garlic, minced

Place bratwurst in saucepan and barely cover with water. Bring to a boil and cook for 5 to 10 minutes; drain well. Cut into bite-size pieces. Thoroughly combine remaining ingredients in Crock-Pot. Add partially cooked bratwurst. Cover and cook on Low setting for 6 to 10 hours. Serve on wooden picks; accompany with plenty of napkins and a good dark bread.

10 to 12 servings (about 2 ½ quarts).

NOTE: If precooked bratwurst sausages are used, omit par-boiling; cut into bite-size pieces and add to sauce.

Polynesian Barbecued Pork

½ cup soy sauce	½ cup barbecue sauce
¼ cup dry sherry	1 can (8 oz.) pineapple chunks, undrained
½ cup brown sugar	3 lb. extra-lean pork, cut into strips, browned and drained
2 cloves garlic, crushed	
⅛ teaspoon pepper	

Combine all ingredients except pork strips in Crock-Pot; stir well. Add pork strips and stir to coat thoroughly. Cover and cook on Low setting for 8 to 10 hours. Serve with a small dish of the sauce for dunking.

15 servings (about 2 ½ quarts).

NOTE: Pork tenderloin is ideal for this recipe.

Party Mix

2 cups O-shaped oat cereal
3 cups bite-size rice cereal
2 cups bite-size shredded wheat cereal
1 cup peanuts, pecans or cashews
1 cup thin pretzel sticks (optional)

½ cup butter or margarine, melted
4 tablespoons Worcestershire sauce
Dash Tabasco sauce
½ teaspoon seasoned salt
½ teaspoon garlic salt
½ teaspoon onion salt

Combine cereals, nuts and pretzels in Crock-Pot. Mix melted butter with all remaining ingredients; pour over cereal mixture in Crock-Pot and toss lightly to coat. *Do not cover Crock-Pot.* Cook on High setting for 2 hours, stirring well every 30 minutes; then turn to Low setting for 2 to 6 hours. Store in airtight container.

Makes 10 cups (about 2½ quarts).

Orange-Cider Punch

1 cup sugar
2 cinnamon sticks
1 whole nutmeg
2 cups apple cider or apple juice

6 cups orange juice
2 cups vodka (optional)

Mix all ingredients except vodka in Crock-Pot; stir well. Cover and cook on Low setting for 4 to 10 hours (on High setting for 2 to 3 hours). Just before serving, stir in vodka. Serve hot, in punch cups.

10 to 15 servings (about 2½ quarts).

Hot Spiced Wine

2 bottles dry red wine	2 cinnamon sticks
3 apples, peeled, cored and thinly sliced	½ cup sugar
3 whole cloves	1 teaspoon lemon juice

Combine all ingredients in Crock-Pot; stir well. Cover and cook on Low setting for 4 to 12 hours (on High setting for 1 to 2 hours). Serve hot, in punch cups or mugs.

6 to 8 servings (about 2 quarts).

Hot Cranberry Punch

4 cups unsweetened pineapple juice	1 cup water
4 cups cranberry juice	1 teaspoon whole cloves and 1 cinnamon stick tied in cheesecloth
½ cup brown sugar (packed)	1 to 2 cups vodka

Combine all ingredients except vodka in Crock-Pot. Cover and cook on Low setting for 4 to 10 hours. Add vodka before serving. Serve hot, in punch cups.

10 to 15 servings (about 2½ quarts).

KEEPING THE HEAT ON

Your Crock-Pot makes an ideal server for a hot punch or hot dip. Keep it on the Low setting to maintain the proper serving temperature. (Creamy dips, however, should not be left uncovered for more than 2 hours.)

DIETER'S FARE

A delicately sauced salmon loaf, a hearty hamburger soup,
peppers stuffed with tuna—can this be the stuff
of which diets are made? Indeed.
These calorie-calculated recipes are especially designed
to please the palate and help control the waistline.
And they're so nondiet-tasting,
the whole family will happily join the low-calorie bandwagon.
With temptations like these,
why put off till tomorrow what should be started today?

Sweet 'n Sour Chicken

3 medium potatoes, peeled and thinly sliced	1 teaspoon leaf basil
4 whole chicken breasts (about 3 pounds), skinned and halved	¼ teaspoon nutmeg
	2 tablespoons cider vinegar
	Dried parsley flakes
1 cup orange juice	1 can (17 oz.) water-packed peach slices, drained
2 tablespoons brown sugar	Chopped parsley

Place sliced potatoes in Crock-Pot. Arrange chicken breasts on potatoes. Combine orange juice, brown sugar, basil, nutmeg and vinegar. Pour over chicken. Sprinkle chicken with dried parsley flakes. Cover and cook on Low setting for 8 to 10 hours.

Remove chicken breasts and potatoes from sauce and arrange on a warm platter. Turn Crock-Pot to High setting. Add peach slices to sauce. Heat until serving temperature. Pour sauce over chicken and potatoes. Garnish with chopped parsley.

8 servings (162 calories per serving).

Chicken Cacciatore

3 whole chicken breasts, skinned and halved
1 teaspoon salt
Dash pepper
1 tablespoon dried onion flakes
1 green pepper, seeded and finely chopped
1 clove garlic, finely chopped
1 can (15 oz.) whole tomatoes, mashed
1 can (4 oz.) sliced mushrooms, drained
2 teaspoons tomato paste
1 bay leaf
¼ teaspoon leaf thyme
2 tablespoons finely chopped pimiento

Wash chicken pieces well and pat dry. Combine remaining ingredients in Crock-Pot. Add chicken pieces, pushing down into liquid to thoroughly moisten and coat. Cover and cook on Low setting for 7 to 9 hours.

6 servings (120 calories per serving).

Low-Cal Meat Loaf

1 lb. lean ground beef
2 cups shredded cabbage
1 medium green pepper, seeded and shredded
1 teaspoon salt
1 tablespoon dried onion flakes
½ teaspoon caraway seed (optional)

Thoroughly combine all ingredients. Shape into round loaf. Place accessory Meat Rack in Crock-Pot. Place meat loaf on rack. Cover and cook on High setting for 4 to 6 hours.

6 servings (106 calories per 3-oz. serving). Recipe may be doubled for larger Crock-Pot.

Hamburger Soup

1½ lb. lean ground beef
1 medium onion, chopped
1 cup sliced pared carrots
1 cup sliced celery
1 cup sliced cabbage

1 can (6 oz.) tomato paste
2 teaspoons Worcester-
shire sauce
3 cups beef bouillon

In skillet, brown hamburger; drain thoroughly. Add onion, carrots, celery and cabbage. Combine tomato paste, Worcestershire sauce and beef bouillon. Add to Crock-Pot and stir to blend. Cover and cook on Low setting for 8 to 10 hours (on High setting for 3 to 4 hours).

8 servings (142 calories per 1-cup serving).

Peppers and Steak

2 lb. lean round steak,
1 inch thick
2 green peppers, seeded
and cut into ½-inch
strips

1 cup beef bouillon
¼ cup soy sauce
½ teaspoon ground ginger
½ teaspoon garlic powder

Cut steak into serving portions. Place half the steak in Crock-Pot. Arrange green peppers on steak. Place remaining steak on top. Mix remaining ingredients and pour over meat. Cover and cook on Low setting for 8 to 10 hours (on High setting for 4 to 5 hours).

6 servings (186 calories per 4-oz. serving).

Veal Loaf

1½ lb. ground veal	1 tablespoon dry minced
1 cup French-style green	onion
beans, chopped	2 tablespoons chopped
1 can (2 oz.) mushrooms,	pimiento
drained and chopped	⅓ cup tomato paste
1½ teaspoons salt	Paprika
¼ teaspoon freshly ground	
pepper	

Mix all ingredients except paprika together well. Shape into loaf. Sprinkle top with paprika. Place on accessory Meat Rack. Cover and cook on Low setting for 8 to 10 hours.

7 servings (138 calories per 3-oz. serving).

Beef Loaf: Substitute lean ground beef for the veal.

Dieter's Chili

2½ lb. ground veal or lean	1 teaspoon salt
ground beef	3 cloves garlic, minced
2 tablespoons dry minced	2 teaspoons monosodium
onion	glutamate
1½ tablespoons chili	1 can (6 oz.) tomato paste
powder (or more)	1½ cups tomato juice
½ teaspoon freshly ground	1 can (16 oz.) chili beans,
pepper	drained (optional)

Brown meat in nonstick skillet; drain thoroughly on absorbent towels. Mix all ingredients in Crock-Pot. Cover and cook on Low setting for 7 to 9 hours. (If you prefer a thinner consistency, more liquid can be added.)

6 servings (336 calories per serving, 270 calories without chili beans).

Polynesian Veal

2 lb. boneless veal
  shoulder, cut into
  1-inch cubes
¾ cup water
¼ cup dry sherry

2 tablespoons soy sauce
1 teaspoon ground ginger
1 teaspoon artificial
  sweetener

Brown veal in nonstick skillet. Mix remaining ingredients in Crock-Pot. Stir in veal. Cover and cook on Low setting for 6 to 8 hours.

4 servings (214 calories per 1-cup serving).

Tuna Casserole

2 cans (7 oz. each) tuna,
  water packed or
  rinsed and drained
1½ cups cooked macaroni
½ cup finely chopped
  onion
¼ cup finely chopped
  green pepper

1 can (4 oz.) sliced mushrooms, drained
1 package (10 oz.) frozen
  cauliflower, partially
  thawed
½ cup chicken bouillon
1 tablespoon diet
  margarine

Combine all ingredients in Crock-Pot; stir well. Cover and cook on Low setting for 7 to 9 hours (on High setting for 3 to 4 hours).

6 servings (178 calories per 1-cup serving).

Poached Fish

1½ to 2 lb. frozen firm-
    textured fish fillets,
    thawed
2 onions, thinly sliced
1 lemon, thinly sliced
2 tablespoons butter,
    melted

2 teaspoons salt
1 bay leaf
4 whole peppercorns
3 cups water
    Avocado Sauce (below)

Cut fillets into serving portions. Combine onion and lemon slices with butter, salt, bay leaf and peppercorns; pour into Crock-Pot. Place fillets on top of onion and lemon slices. Add water. Cover and cook on High setting for 3 to 4 hours.

Before serving, carefully remove fish fillets with slotted spoon or spatula. Place on heatproof platter. Sprinkle with juice of ½ lemon. Garnish with additional lemon slices. Serve hot with Avocado Sauce, or chill and serve cold.

6 servings (245 calories per serving; 145 calories without sauce).

AVOCADO SAUCE

1 can (7½ oz.) frozen
    avocado dip, thawed
½ cup sour cream

2 tablespoons lemon juice
½ small onion, finely
    chopped

Combine all ingredients and mix well.

Salmon Loaf with Crab Sauce

1 can (16 oz.) salmon,
   drained, flaked and
   boned
2 slices bread, crumbed
½ cup evaporated skim
   milk
1 egg

¼ cup chicken bouillon
¼ cup finely chopped
   celery
½ teaspoon onion salt
   Crab Sauce (below)
   Dash paprika or cayenne
   pepper

Coat Crock-Pot with spray-on nonstick vegetable coating. Mix thoroughly all ingredients except Crab Sauce and paprika and pour into Crock-Pot. Cover and cook on High setting for 3 to 5 hours.

Serve salmon loaf on warm platter with Crab Sauce poured over. Garnish with paprika.

4 servings (255 calories per 6-oz. serving; 237 calories without sauce).

CRAB SAUCE

1 can (6 oz.) Alaska King
   crabmeat, drained, flaked
   and cartilage removed

¼ cup chicken broth or
   clam juice
1 tablespoon lemon juice

Mix sauce ingredients well, tossing crabmeat with liquid to coat and separate.

NO MEAT RACK?

Many of the recipes in this section call for the use of the accessory Meat Rack to keep the food elevated, away from the fat and juices. Write to Rival Manufacturing Company for ordering information.

Flounder with Herbs

2 lb. flounder fillets (fresh or frozen)
1 teaspoon salt
¾ cup chicken bouillon
2 tablespoons lemon juice
4 tablespoons fresh chopped parsley

2 tablespoons dried chives
2 tablespoons dry minced onion
½ to 1 teaspoon leaf marjoram

Wipe fish as dry as possible and sprinkle with salt. Cut into portions to fit Crock-Pot. Combine bouillon and lemon juice; stir in remaining ingredients. Place accessory Meat Rack in Crock-Pot. Layer fish on rack, pouring liquid mixture over each portion. Cover and cook on High setting for 3 to 4 hours.

6 servings (110 calories per 4-oz. serving).

Tuna-Stuffed Peppers

2 cups tomato juice
1 can (6 oz.) tomato paste
2 cans (7 oz. each) chunk-style tuna, drained and rinsed
2 tablespoons dried onion flakes

2 tablespoons dried vegetable flakes
Garlic powder
4 medium green peppers, tops removed and seeded

Mix tomato juice and tomato paste; reserve 1 cup. Mix remaining tomato juice mixture with remaining ingredients except peppers. Fill the peppers equally with mixture and place in Crock-Pot. Pour the reserved 1 cup tomato juice mixture over peppers. Cover and cook on Low setting for 8 to 9 hours.

4 servings (195 calories per serving).

Herbed Zucchini

2 lb. zucchini (unpeeled), sliced
2 chicken bouillon cubes
1¼ teaspoons salt
½ teaspoon garlic salt
2 tablespoons dried onion flakes
2 teaspoons dried parsley flakes
¼ teaspoon leaf oregano
1 cup tomato juice

Mix all ingredients together carefully in Crock-Pot. Cover and cook on High setting for 3 to 4 hours. If a thicker sauce is desired, remove cover during last hour.

6 servings (40 calories per 1-cup serving).

Lima Bean Soup

1 package (10 oz.) frozen lima beans
2 chicken bouillon cubes
1½ cups boiling water
½ cup finely chopped pared carrots
¼ cup chopped onion
¼ cup chopped celery
¼ cup chopped green pepper
Dash leaf basil
Dash leaf thyme
Salt and pepper

Cook lima beans as directed on package; drain. Dissolve bouillon cubes in boiling water; cool. Combine lima beans and bouillon in blender container; blend until smooth. Pour into Crock-Pot. Add remaining ingredients. Cover and cook on Low setting for 6 to 10 hours (on High setting for 2 to 3 hours).

4 servings (88 calories per 1-cup serving). Double recipe for 5-quart Crock-Pot.

GAMESMANSHIP

The Crock-Pot's slow and steady cooking pace takes
the wild right out of game ... even the toughest critter
can be tamed into a tender, tempting dish.
Use these recipes to do justice to the hunter's bounty.
(But make sure the hunter has done his part.
Even the Crock-Pot can't work miracles
on game that's been improperly dressed.)

Rabbit in Cream

1 large or 2 small rabbits,
　cut up
3 tablespoons minced ham
　or bacon
1 onion, finely chopped
½ teaspoon leaf thyme
1 can (4 oz.) sliced mush-
　rooms, drained

1 cup beef bouillon
1 cup sour cream
2 tablespoons lemon juice
3 tablespoons flour
　Minced parsley

Marinate rabbit overnight in refrigerator in salted water. Before cooking, remove rabbit pieces; drain and pat dry. Place rabbit, ham, onion, thyme and mushrooms in Crock-Pot. Pour in bouillon, moistening well. Cover and cook on Low setting for 8 to 10 hours.

Before serving, turn to High setting. Combine sour cream, lemon juice and flour. Remove rabbit to a warm platter. Stir sour cream mixture into juices in Crock-Pot. Cook until thickened. Spoon sauce over rabbit and sprinkle with parsley.

6 servings (about 3 quarts).

Squirrel in Cream: Substitute 2 small squirrels, cut-up, for the rabbit.

Hasenpfeffer

2½- to 3-lb. rabbit, cut up	1 tablespoon salt
2 cups dry red wine	1 teaspoon whole cloves
2 tablespoons wine	⅛ teaspoon pepper
vinegar	2 bay leaves
1 tablespoon sugar	

Place cut-up rabbit in flat refrigerator container. In bowl, combine remaining ingredients; pour over rabbit. Marinate overnight in refrigerator. Place marinated rabbit in Crock-Pot. Add 1½ cups marinade. Cover and cook on Low setting for 8 to 10 hours.

Remove meat to warm platter. Thicken gravy, if desired.

4 servings (about 3 quarts).

Venison Stew

2 to 3 lb. venison, cut into 1-inch cubes	3 stalks celery, cut into 1-inch pieces
1½ cups French dressing	1 can (16 oz.) whole tomatoes, mashed
2 carrots, pared and cut into 1-inch pieces	¼ cup quick-cooking tapioca
1 large onion, coarsely chopped	1 whole clove
1 small green pepper, seeded and coarsely chopped	1 bay leaf
	Salt and pepper

Marinate cubed venison in French dressing for 12 to 24 hours in refrigerator. Drain off salad dressing and place venison in Crock-Pot. Stir in remaining ingredients. Cover and cook on Low setting for 8 to 10 hours.

6 to 8 servings (about 3 quarts).

Barbecued Venison

2- to 3-lb. venison round,
    leg or rump roast
1 can (12 oz.) beer
3 cloves garlic
    Salt and pepper

2 onions, sliced
3 bay leaves
2 cups Barbecue Sauce
    (below)

Trim excess fat from venison. In large bowl, mix beer, garlic, salt, pepper, onions and bay leaves; add venison. (Marinade should cover meat.) Marinate in refrigerator for 12 to 24 hours, turning occasionally. Remove venison and onions from marinade and place in Crock-Pot. Pour 1 cup Barbecue Sauce over top. Cover and cook on Low setting for 10 to 12 hours.

6 servings (about 3 quarts).

BARBECUE SAUCE

1 cup finely chopped
    onion
¾ cup finely chopped
    celery
3 tablespoons butter
6 tablespoons sugar
3 tablespoons Worcester-
    shire sauce

6 tablespoons wine vinegar
¼ cup lemon juice
3 cups ketchup
3 teaspoons dry mustard
2 teaspoons liquid hickory
    smoke
Salt and pepper

In skillet, sauté onion and celery in butter. Add to Crock-Pot with remaining ingredients. Cover and cook on Low setting for 8 to 10 hours (on High setting for 3 to 4 hours, stirring occasionally).

5 cups (about 1½ quarts).

NOTE: This sauce can be doubled, if desired; it freezes well, too.

Braised Pheasant

2 pheasants (about 1½ lb. each) or 1 pheasant (3 lb.), split	2 carrots, pared and quartered
Salt and pepper	2 slices lean smoked bacon
1 onion, sliced	¼ cup chicken broth
	¼ cup dry sherry or broth

Season cavity of each pheasant lightly with salt and pepper. Arrange sliced vegetables in bottom of Crock-Pot. Place pheasants on top of vegetables. Cut bacon slices in half and place over each breast. Add broth and sherry. Cover and cook on Low setting for 8 to 10 hours (on High setting for 3 to 4 hours).

2 to 4 servings (about 3 quarts).

Quail in Wine-Herb Sauce

12 quail	1 can (4 oz.) sliced mushrooms, drained
3 tablespoons flour	1 bay leaf
Salt and pepper	½ teaspoon leaf thyme
1 large onion, sliced	½ cup beef broth
2 slices lean smoked bacon, diced	½ cup dry white wine
1 clove garlic, crushed	Chopped parsley

Coat quail with a mixture of the flour, salt and pepper. Place onion slices in Crock-Pot; top with quail. Cover quail with diced bacon. Add remaining ingredients except parsley. Cover and cook on Low setting for 7 to 9 hours.

Remove quail to a heated platter and sprinkle with parsley. Thicken sauce, if desired, and spoon over quail.

6 servings (about 3 quarts).

FOR THE TWOSOME

**Especially developed for today's lifestyles,
all of these recipes are economically and efficiently sized
for coping with one, two . . . or just a few.
Of course, they can also be prepared in larger quantities—
and even doubled, if the pot permits.
Use these ingredient amounts as your guide for tailoring
other recipes in this book to small-size servings.**

Company Beef

1 medium onion, thinly sliced
¼ cup butter
1½ lb. stewing beef, cut into 1½-inch cubes
Salt and pepper
1 bay leaf
1 tablespoon dried currants
3 tablespoons tomato paste
¼ cup red Burgundy wine
1 tablespoon wine vinegar
1 tablespoon brown sugar
Dash garlic powder
⅛ teaspoon cinnamon
⅛ teaspoon cumin
Dash ground cloves
¼ lb. Monterey Jack cheese, diced or grated
¼ cup walnuts

In skillet, sauté onion in butter until limp. Season beef with salt and pepper; add to skillet and stir to coat beef with onion and butter. Place in Crock-Pot. Stir together remaining ingredients except cheese and walnuts and add to beef. Cover and cook on Low setting for 8 to 10 hours (on High setting for 3 to 5 hours). Stir to blend. Sprinkle with diced or grated cheese and walnuts and cook on Low setting for an additional 15 minutes.

Spicy Cabbage Rolls

6 large cabbage leaves
2 tablespoons water
¼ cup minced onion
½ lb. lean ground chuck
1 tablespoon ketchup
1 small egg, lightly beaten
2 tablespoons raw long-
   grain converted rice
½ teaspoon salt
⅛ teaspoon pepper

1 can (8 oz.) stewed
   tomatoes
2 tablespoons raisins
2 tablespoons cider vinegar
2 tablespoons brown sugar
2 tablespoons dark corn
   syrup
½ cup crumbled ginger-
   snaps

In saucepan, immerse cabbage leaves in enough boiling water to cover and simmer for about 5 minutes or until pliable. Remove from water carefully and drain. In bowl, make stuffing by combining water, onion, ground chuck, ketchup, egg, rice, salt and pepper. Cut out heavy ribs from the cabbage leaves. Divide stuffing into 6 equal portions; place a portion in center of each cabbage leaf and fold the leaf around it. Secure with a wooden toothpick. Place the rolls seam side down in the Crock-Pot.

Combine remaining ingredients except gingersnaps and pour over cabbage rolls. Cover and cook on Low setting for 8 to 10 hours.

Remove rolls to warm serving platter. Add crumbled ginger-snaps to sauce and cook on Low setting for an additional 15 minutes. Spoon sauce over rolls before serving.

2 or 3 servings (about 1½ quarts).

Simply Stew

1 package (24 oz.) frozen
stew vegetables
1 lb. lean stewing beef,
cut into 1½-inch cubes
1 can (10¾ oz.) condensed
tomato soup

½ cup water
2 tablespoons dried onion
flakes
1 teaspoon salt
¼ teaspoon pepper
1 bay leaf

Place vegetables in bottom of Crock-Pot. Add meat. In separate bowl, mix remaining ingredients and pour over meat and vegetables. Cover and cook on Low setting for 12 to 14 hours (on High setting for 3 to 4 hours).

4 servings (1½ to 2 quarts).

NOTE: This stew freezes well.

Curried Lamb Stew

¾ lb. boneless lean lamb,
cut into ½-inch cubes
1 apple, cored and
chopped
1 cup chopped celery
½ cup chopped onion
3 tablespoons butter
3 tablespoons flour

1 teaspoon curry powder
2 cups chicken broth
½ cup raw long-grain
converted rice
½ teaspoon salt
Dash pepper
Thin lemon slices

In skillet, brown lamb, apple, celery and onion in butter. Stir in flour and curry powder. Turn mixture into Crock-Pot. Add broth, rice, salt and pepper; stir well. Cover and cook on Low setting for 8 to 10 hours. Serve garnished with lemon slices.

4 servings (1½ to 2 quarts).

Ham and Sweet Potatoes

2 to 4 small sweet potatoes (unpeeled)	¼ cup brown sugar
1½-lb. boneless ham	½ teaspoon dry mustard

Place sweet potatoes in bottom of Crock-Pot. Place ham on sweet potatoes (the sweet potatoes act as a rack). Combine remaining ingredients and spread over top of ham. Cover and cook on Low setting for 8 to 10 hours.

To serve, slice ham and sweet potatoes and pour juices over top.

2 to 4 servings (about 2 quarts).

Ham and Vegetables

2 medium potatoes, peeled and cut up	½ teaspoon salt
1 lb. green beans, cut up	1 lb. lean cooked ham, cut up
1½ cups water	

Place ingredients in Crock-Pot in order given. Cover and cook on High setting for 4 to 6 hours.

2 or 3 servings (1½ to 2 quarts).

Ham and Noodle Casserole

1 cup uncooked noodles
  Vegetable oil
1 cup cubed cooked ham
1 can (10¾ oz.) condensed
  cream of chicken soup
1 can (8 oz.) whole-kernel
  corn, drained

1 tablespoon chopped
  pimiento
½ cup grated Cheddar
  cheese
¼ cup chopped green
  pepper

Cook noodles according to package directions until barely tender; drain and toss with just enough oil to coat. Add noodles and remaining ingredients to greased Crock-Pot; stir to mix. Cover and cook on Low setting for 7 to 9 hours.

2 servings (1½ to 2 quarts).

Soup 'n Sausage

½ cup lentils
½ lb. Polish sausage, sliced
1 cup minced onion
½ cup chopped pared
  carrots
½ cup chopped celery
1 can (16 oz.) tomato
  sauce

2 cups water
  Pinch leaf basil
  Pinch leaf marjoram
1 bay leaf
½ teaspoon salt

Completely soften beans as directed on page 100. In skillet, brown sliced sausage; drain well. Combine softened lentils and browned sausage in Crock-Pot. Add remaining ingredients and stir to mix. Cover and cook on Low setting for 10 to 12 hours (on High setting for 4 to 5 hours). Taste for seasoning.

4 servings (1½ to 2 quarts).

Chicken Creole

---

4 to 6 chicken thighs, legs
   or breasts
Paprika
Salt and pepper
½ cup chopped onion
½ cup chopped green
   pepper
¼ cup chopped celery

1 can (8 oz.) stewed
   tomatoes
1 can (4 oz.) sliced mushrooms, drained
¼ teaspoon leaf thyme
2 tablespoons quick-
   cooking tapioca
Fluffy rice

Sprinkle chicken with paprika, salt and pepper. Broil for
about 15 minutes or until browned; drain. Place browned
chicken in Crock-Pot. Mix remaining ingredients except rice
and pour over Chicken. Cover and cook on Low setting for
7 to 9 hours (on High setting for 3 to 4 hours).

Remove chicken from sauce before serving; serve sauce
over hot fluffy rice.

2 servings (1 ½ to 2 quarts).

Chicken and Rice Casserole

---

1 can (10¾ oz.) condensed
   cream of celery soup
1 can (2 oz.) sliced mushrooms, undrained
½ cup raw long-grain
   converted rice

2 chicken breasts, halved,
   skinned and boned
1 tablespoon dry onion
   soup mix

Combine soup, mushrooms and rice in greased Crock-Pot;
stir well. Lay chicken breasts on top of mixture and sprinkle
with onion soup mix. Cover and cook on Low setting for
7 to 9 hours.

2 servings (1 ½ to 2 quarts).

GROUP GATHERINGS

Good things don't always come in small packages.
And here, as testimony, is a collection of recipes
tailored to the 6-quart Crock-Pot.
Some of these recipes are of the big-batch variety—
perfect for a crowd-size party.
Others treat those meats that are just too big
for the smaller-sized Crock-Pots.
Using these recipes as your guide, you can double many
of the recipes from other chapters in the book.

Braised Leg of Lamb

4- to 5-lb. leg of lamb,
   boned, trimmed, rolled
   and tied
2 to 3 cloves garlic,
   slivered
2 teaspoons salt
¼ teaspoon pepper
½ teaspoon leaf thyme
   Pinch cinnamon
Pinch fennel seed
1 to 2 onions, sliced
1 to 2 carrots, pared and
   sliced
1 stalk celery with leaves,
   sliced
1 sprig parsley
1 cup beef broth

Make slits in lamb with knife and insert garlic slivers. Season
lamb with salt, pepper, thyme, cinnamon and fennel. Place
onions, carrots, celery and parsley in Crock-Pot. Add rolled
lamb and beef broth. Cover and cook on High setting for 1 hour.
Turn to Low setting and cook 10 to 12 hours.

Remove lamb to warm serving platter. Broth may be thickened with a flour-water paste or served as is with lamb and
vegetables.

8 to 10 servings (about 4 quarts).

Leg of Lamb Provençale

4- to 5-lb. leg of lamb,
shank removed
Salt and pepper
2 cloves garlic, slivered
2 onions, sliced

2 anchovy fillets, cut into
1-inch pieces
(optional)
½ cup beef broth

Trim excess fat from lamb. Lightly season with salt and pepper. Make slits with a knife into bone area; insert garlic slivers. Place sliced onions in bottom of Crock-Pot. Place lamb on top of onions. Lay anchovy fillets over top of lamb. Add broth. Cover and cook on High setting for 1 hour. Turn to Low setting and cook 10 to 12 hours.

12 to 15 servings (about 4 quarts).

Pasta Sauce with Meatballs

Shortening or olive oil
2 cups chopped onion
2½ cups chopped green
pepper
Meatballs (opposite)
1 package (5 oz.) little
smokie sausage links
4 cans (12 oz. each)
tomato paste

4 cans water (use tomato
paste cans)
1 teaspoon garlic
powder
1 tablespoon dried
parsley flakes
½ teaspoon salt
1 cup grated Romano
cheese

In large skillet, heat shortening to ½-inch depth. Brown onion and green pepper together. Remove with slotted spoon and place in Crock-Pot. Brown meatballs in shortening remaining in skillet. Turn carefully to brown all sides. Remove browned meatballs with slotted spoon, draining excess grease. Place in Crock-Pot. Brown sausages in same skillet; drain on absorbent towels. Place in Crock-Pot.

Drain grease from skillet, leaving only enough to coat the bottom. Add tomato paste and cook over low heat to brown (bright red color will become dull red). Stir constantly to prevent burning. Add 2 cans water, 1 can at a time, thoroughly rinsing each can; stir to blend. Pour over meatballs and sausages in Crock-Pot. Add remaining cans water to Crock-Pot.

Add remaining ingredients; blend carefully so as not to tear meatballs. Cover and cook on High setting for 4 to 6 hours, stirring occasionally (or on Low setting for 8 to 12 hours).

12 to 15 servings (about 4½ quarts).

NOTE: This recipe may be halved for the 3½–quart Crock-Pot. (Cook on Low setting for 8 to 10 hours).

MEATBALLS

2½ to 3 lb. ground chuck or lean ground beef	1 to 2 teaspoons garlic powder
1½ cups grated Romano cheese	4 teaspoons dried parsley flakes
3 eggs	1 teaspoon salt
⅔ cup dry bread crumbs	

Mix all ingredients well and shape into 30 to 36 meatballs about 1½ inches in diameter.

Rolled Rib Roast

4- to 5-lb. rolled beef rib roast	Salt and pepper
Kitchen Bouquet	1 clove garlic
	Yorkshire Pudding (below)

Trim off excess fat from roast, leaving a 1/16-inch or less layer. Generously coat roast with Kitchen Bouquet. Sprinkle with salt and pepper. Insert garlic clove into fat and meat. Place the accessory Meat Rack in bottom of Crock-Pot to elevate meat. Place meat on rack with fat side up. Cover and cook on Low setting for 10 to 12 hours.

One hour before serving, remove roast to heatproof platter. Preheat oven to 425°. Pour juices and fat drippings from Crock-Pot and reserve.

Skim 1 cup of fat drippings into a baking dish, about 8×14 inches, and allow to heat while oven is preheating. Prepare Yorkshire Pudding. Pour into preheated baking dish; mix well with hot fat. Bake for 15 to 20 minutes until firm. Cut into squares or rectangles and serve with roast beef.

8 to 10 servings (about 4 quarts).

YORKSHIRE PUDDING

3 eggs	1 teaspoon salt
1 cup milk	1 tablespoon dried
1½ cups flour	parsley flakes

Beat eggs with milk. Stir in flour, salt and parsley flakes; mix until just smooth.

Famous Chili

½ lb. dried pinto or kidney beans
2 cans (28 oz. each) whole tomatoes
2 large green peppers, seeded and coarsely chopped
2 medium onions, coarsely chopped
2 cloves garlic, crushed
½ cup finely chopped parsley
2 lb. lean ground beef
1 lb. lean ground pork
2 to 3 tablespoons chili powder
Salt
1 teaspoon pepper
1 teaspoon cumin seed

Completely soften beans as directed on page 100. Simmer until softened. Drain and place in Crock-Pot; add tomatoes, green peppers, onions, garlic and parsley. In a large skillet, saute the beef and pork for about 15 minutes to remove excess fat. Drain and add meats to other ingredients in Crock-Pot. Season with chili powder, salt, pepper and cumin seed; mix thoroughly. Cover and cook on Low setting for 8 to 14 hours (on High setting for 4 to 5½ hours).

One hour before serving, taste for seasoning and add additional chili powder if necessary.

12 servings (about 4 quarts).

Cornish Hens Basque

4 Rock Cornish hens
   (about 16 oz. each)
¼ cup flour
2 teaspoons salt
½ teaspoon pepper
¼ teaspoon chili powder
2 small onions, sliced
2 cups cubed peeled
   eggplant
1 green pepper, seeded
   and cut into ½-inch
   strips

4 oz. mushrooms, sliced
1 jar (2 oz.) chopped
   pimiento
1 clove garlic, chopped
1 tablespoon olive oil
1 large bay leaf
½ teaspoon leaf thyme
1 teaspoon leaf basil
1 teaspoon salt
½ teaspoon pepper
¾ cup dry white wine or
   chicken broth

Rinse hens and pat dry. Mix flour, 2 teaspoons salt, ½ teaspoon pepper and chili powder. Coat hens with flour mixture. Combine onions, eggplant, green pepper, mushrooms, pimiento, garlic and oil in Crock-Pot. Arrange hens on top of vegetables. Sprinkle with remaining seasonings. Pour wine over hens. Cover and cook on Low setting for 8 to 10 hours. Just before serving, taste sauce for seasoning.

4 to 8 servings (about 4 quarts). Halve recipe for smaller Crock-Pots.

Duckling with Orange Sauce

3½- to 4-lb. domestic duck	2 cloves garlic
Salt and pepper	2 cups water
1 orange (unpeeled), sliced	Orange Sauce (below)
1 small onion, sliced	

Rinse duck well and pat dry. Prick skin in several places with a fork. Sprinkle cavity generously with salt and pepper. Place orange slices, onion slices and garlic in Crock-Pot. Place duck on top; add water. Cover and cook on Low setting for 8 to 10 hours (or on High setting for 3½ to 5 hours or until tender).

Before serving, remove duck to a heatproof platter; wipe and prick skin again. Pour off all fat and liquid. Brush duck with Orange Sauce. Roast duck in preheated 425° oven for 20 to 30 minutes to brown and crisp, basting occasionally with the sauce.

2 to 4 servings (about 4½ quarts).

ORANGE SAUCE

1 cup orange marmalade	2 tablespoons orange-flavored liqueur
½ cup orange juice	
2 tablespoons freshly grated orange peel	

Combine all ingredients in small saucepan. Heat over low heat, stirring until smooth.

Boiled Ham

3- to 4-lb. smoked ham
   shank
Salt

1 bay leaf
4 or 5 peppercorns
2 cups water

Place ham in Crock-Pot. Add seasonings and pour in water. Cover and cook on Low setting for 8 to 12 hours.

8 servings (about 4½ quarts).

Green Tomato Mincemeat

2 lb. green tomatoes
2 lb. apples, cored
¼ lb. suet
1½ tablespoons salt
1½ tablespoons cinnamon
4 tablespoons grated
   lemon peel

½ cup lemon juice
½ cup orange juice
2 cups raisins
7 cups sugar
1 teaspoon cloves
1 teaspoon nutmeg

Put tomatoes, apples and suet through grinder. Combine all ingredients in Crock-Pot; stir well. Cover and cook on High setting for 4 to 6 hours. Stir occasionally. Remove cover during last 2 hours of cooking. Ladle into hot sterilized jars and pressure can according to standard canning methods.

8 to 10 half-pint jars (about 4 quarts). Halve recipe for 3½-quart Crock-Pot. Cooking time remains the same.

BREADS, CAKES AND SUCH

Yeast breads and tea breads, cakes and puddings,
brownies and compotes. With reasons like these,
isn't it high time you thought about putting
your Crock-Pot to work as a bakery? The aroma alone is worth it.
And the home-baked results will make store-bought goods
seem never quite good enough again.
What's more, many of these breads and bakings
lend themselves particularly well to freezing.
When cool, just wrap, label and freeze—for up to 3 months.
By doing your baking at times when you have better things to do,
you can build up a "fresh-baked" inventory
ready to earn you "How do you do it?" compliments.

White Bread

---

1 package active dry yeast	1 cup lukewarm water
1 teaspoon sugar	1 teaspoon salt
¼ cup warm water	¼ cup sugar
1 egg	3½ to 4 cups flour
¼ cup vegetable oil	

In large bowl, dissolve yeast and 1 teaspoon sugar in ¼ cup warm water. Allow to stand until it bubbles and foams. Add egg, oil, lukewarm water, salt, ¼ cup sugar and 2 cups of the flour. Beat with an electric mixer for 2 minutes. With wooden spoon, stir in remaining 1½ to 2 cups flour until dough leaves the side of the bowl. Place dough in well-greased Bread 'n Cake Bake pan; cover. Place pan in Crock-Pot. Cover and bake on High setting for 2 to 3 hours or until edges are browned.

Remove pan and uncover. Let stand 5 minutes. Unmold on cake rack.

1 loaf (for 3½– or 5–quart Crock-Pot).

Honey Wheat Bread

---

2 cups warm reconsti- tuted dry milk	¾ teaspoon salt
2 tablespoons vegetable oil	1 package active dry yeast
	3 cups whole wheat flour
¼ cup honey	¾ to 1 cup all-purpose flour

Combine warm (not hot) milk, oil, honey, salt, yeast and half the flour. With electric mixer, beat well for about

2 minutes. Add remaining flour; mix well. Place dough in well-greased Bread 'n Cake Bake pan; cover. Let stand for 5 minutes. Place pan in Crock-Pot. Cover and bake on High setting for 2 to 3 hours.

Remove pan and uncover. Let stand 5 minutes. Unmold and serve warm.

1 loaf (for 3½- or 5-quart Crock-Pot).

NOTE: Fresh milk may be used if scalded.

Health Bread

---

1 package active dry yeast	¼ cup brown sugar
¼ cup warm water	(packed)
1 cup milk, scalded	¼ cup wheat germ
½ cup rolled oats	½ cup rye flour
1 teaspoon salt	1 cup whole wheat flour
2 tablespoons vegetable	1¼ to 1½ cups unbleached
oil	all-purpose flour
1 egg	

Dissolve yeast in warm water. In large bowl, pour scalded milk over rolled oats; cool. Add salt, oil, egg, brown sugar, wheat germ, rye flour and whole wheat flour. Stir in yeast mixture. Beat with an electric mixer for 2 minutes. Stir in enough unbleached flour to form a stiff dough or until dough leaves the side of the bowl. Place dough in well-greased Bread 'n Cake Bake pan; cover. Place pan in Crock-Pot. Cover and bake on High setting for 2 to 3 hours or until edges are browned.

Remove pan and uncover. Let stand 5 minutes. Unmold and serve warm.

1 loaf (for 3½- or 5-quart Crock-Pot).

Sourdough Starter

1 package active dry yeast
½ cup lukewarm water
2 cups lukewarm water
2 cups flour
1 tablespoon sugar
1 teaspoon salt

In glass or crockery container, dissolve yeast in ½ cup luke-warm water. Add remaining ingredients and stir well with a wooden or plastic spoon until smooth. Cover with a towel and let stand for 3 to 5 days at room temperature. Stir 2 or 3 times daily. To store, cover and refrigerate.

About 4 cups starter.

Sourdough Bread

1 package active dry yeast
¾ cup warm water
1 teaspoon sugar
½ cup sourdough starter
1 teaspoon salt
2½ to 2¾ cups flour
¼ teaspoon baking soda

Soften yeast in the warm water. Blend in sugar and let stand 10 minutes. Stir in sourdough starter and salt. Add 1½ cups of the flour and beat with an electric mixer for 3 to 4 minutes. Mix 1 cup of the flour with soda and stir into bat-ter. Add remaining flour, if needed, to make a stiff dough. Grease hands and shape dough into loaf (dough will be slightly sticky). Place in well-greased Bread 'n Cake Bake pan; cover. Place in Crock-Pot. Cover and bake on High setting for 2 to 3 hours.

Remove pan and uncover. Let stand for 5 minutes. Unmold on cake rack; brush crust with butter and serve warm.

1 loaf (for 3½- or 5-quart Crock-Pot).

SOURDOUGH TIPS

•Add 1 teaspoon sugar to starter if not used within 10 days.

•To replenish the starter, add ½ cup flour, ½ cup water and 1 teaspoon sugar; stir well. Cover and let stand 1 day at room temperature. To store, cover and refrigerate.

Sourdough Honey Wheat Bread

¾ **cup milk**	1½ **tablespoons wheat germ**
2 **teaspoons butter**	2 **teaspoons sugar**
1½ **tablespoons honey**	1 **teaspoon salt**
1 **package active dry yeast**	½ **teaspoon baking soda**
¾ **cup sourdough starter**	1½ **cups all-purpose flour**
¾ **cup whole wheat flour**	

Scald milk. Add butter and honey to scalded milk; allow to melt and cool to lukewarm. Mix yeast in milk and stir to dissolve. Add the sourdough starter, the whole wheat flour and wheat germ. Blend sugar, salt and soda until smooth and sprinkle over top of dough, stirring in gently. Stir in remaining flour until too stiff to stir. Turn out onto floured board and knead 100 times. Shape into a loaf and place in well-greased Bread 'n Cake Bake pan; cover. Place in Crock-Pot. Cover and bake on High setting for 2 to 3 hours or until edges are browned.

Remove pan and uncover. Let stand 5 minutes. Unmold on cake rack and serve warm.

1 loaf (for 3½– or 5–quart Crock-Pot).

Dilly Casserole Bread

1 package active dry yeast	1 tablespoon instant
¼ cup very warm water	minced onion
1 cup cream-style cottage	2 teaspoons dill seed
cheese, heated to	1 teaspoon salt
lukewarm	¼ teaspoon baking soda
1 tablespoon butter	1 egg
2 tablespoons sugar	2¼ to 2½ cups flour

Soften yeast in warm water. In mixing bowl, combine cottage cheese, butter, sugar, onion, dill seed, salt, soda, egg and the softened yeast. Add flour gradually, beating well after each addition to form a stiff dough. Turn into well-greased Bread 'n Cake Bake pan; cover. Place in Crock-Pot. Cover and bake on High setting for 3 to 4 hours.

Remove pan and uncover. Let stand 5 minutes. Unmold and serve warm.

1 loaf (for 3½– or 5–quart Crock-Pot).

Spoon Bread, Georgia Style

1 cup yellow cornmeal	2 tablespoons vegetable oil
2 teaspoons baking powder	or butter
2 eggs	1 cup buttermilk
1 cup grated sharp cheese	1 to 2 green chili peppers,
1 can (17 oz.) cream-style	seeded and diced
corn	

Mix all ingredients well. Pour into greased and floured Bread 'n Cake Bake pan; cover. Place in Crock-Pot. Cover and bake on High setting for 2 to 3½ hours. Do not unmold. Serve warm, directly from the pan.

4 to 6 servings (for 3½- or 5-quart Crock-Pot).

Lemon Tea Bread

2 cups flour
1½ teaspoons baking
  powder
¼ teaspoon salt
½ cup margarine or butter,
  softened
1 cup sugar

2 eggs
⅓ cup milk
½ cup chopped walnuts
2 teaspoons freshly grated
  lemon peel
Lemon Glaze (below)

Stir together flour, baking powder and salt; set aside. With electric mixer, cream margarine and sugar. Add eggs, one at a time, and beat until fluffy. Beat in flour alternately with milk, beginning and ending with flour, just until blended. With wooden spoon, stir in nuts and lemon peel. Pour into well-greased and floured Bread 'n Cake Bake pan; cover. Place in Crock-Pot. Cover and bake on High setting for 3 to 4 hours or until bread tests done with a wooden pick.

Remove pan and uncover. Unmold on cake rack and cool for 10 minutes. Prepare Lemon Glaze. Prick bread with a fork and pour glaze over bread. Serve warm.

1 loaf (for 3½- or 5-quart Crock-Pot).

LEMON GLAZE

¼ cup lemon juice

⅓ cup sugar

Combine lemon juice and sugar in saucepan. Cook, stirring constantly, for 1 minute or until syrupy.

Pineapple Bread

2¾ cups flour
¾ cup sugar
3 teaspoons baking
  powder
¾ teaspoon salt
1 egg, lightly beaten
⅓ cup milk

⅓ cup butter or margarine,
  melted
1 cup drained crushed
  pineapple
1 cup chopped dates
1 cup chopped walnuts

Stir together flour, sugar, baking powder and salt. In another bowl, combine egg, milk, butter, pineapple, dates and nuts with a wooden spoon. Stir fruit mixture into dry ingredients until moistened. Pour into well-greased and floured Bread 'n Cake Bake pan; cover. Place in Crock-Pot. Cover and bake on High setting for 3 to 4 hours or until bread tests done with a wooden pick.

Remove pan and uncover. Let stand 5 minutes. Unmold on cake rack. To store, wrap in aluminum foil and refrigerate.

1 loaf (for 3½– or 5–quart Crock-Pot).

Cherry-Orange Bread

---

2 cups flour
1 cup sugar
1½ teaspoons baking
  powder
1 teaspoon salt
½ teaspoon baking soda
¼ cup shortening

¾ cup orange juice
1 egg, well beaten
1 cup pitted tart cherries,
  chopped
½ cup chopped nuts

Stir together flour, sugar, baking powder, salt and soda. Cut in shortening with a fork or pastry blender, as you would for pie crust. Combine orange juice and egg; add to dry ingredients, mixing just to moisten. Stir in cherries and nuts. Pour into greased and floured Bread 'n Cake Bake pan; cover. Place in Crock-Pot. Cover and bake on High setting for 3 to 4 hours or until bread tests done with a wooden pick.

Remove pan and uncover. Let stand 5 minutes. Unmold on cake rack. To store, wrap in aluminum foil and refrigerate.

1 loaf (for 3½– or 5–quart Crock-Pot).

Zucchini Bread

2 eggs	¼ teaspoon salt
⅔ cup vegetable oil	½ teaspoon baking
1⅓ cups sugar	powder
1⅓ cups grated peeled	1 teaspoon cinnamon
zucchini	½ teaspoon nutmeg
2 teaspoons vanilla	½ to 1 cup chopped nuts
2 cups flour	

With electric mixer, beat eggs until light and foamy. Add oil, sugar, grated zucchini and vanilla; mix well. Stir dry ingredients together with nuts and add to zucchini mixture; mix well. Pour into greased and floured Bread 'n Cake Bake pan; cover. Place in Crock-Pot. Cover and bake on High setting for 3 to 4 hours or until bread tests done with a wooden pick. Do not check or remove cover until last hour of baking.

Remove pan and uncover. Let stand 5 minutes. Unmold on cake rack. To store, wrap in aluminum foil and refrigerate.

1 loaf (for 3½– or 5–quart Crock-Pot).

Orange Baba

---

1 package active dry yeast	1¾ cups flour
¼ cup very warm water	6 tablespoons butter or
⅓ cup sugar	margarine, softened
½ teaspoon salt	Orange Sauce (below)
3 eggs	

In mixing bowl, sprinkle yeast over warm water; stir until dissolved. Add sugar, salt, eggs and 1¼ cups of the flour; beat with electric mixer until smooth. Add softened butter and beat until well blended, about 3 minutes. Gradually beat in remaining ½ cup flour. Continue to beat until smooth, using a wooden spoon if batter becomes too thick. Pour into greased and floured Bread 'n Cake Bake pan and allow to rise 30 minutes while preheating Crock-Pot on High setting. Cover pan and place in Crock-Pot. Cover and bake on High setting for 2 hours or until done.

Remove pan and uncover. Let stand for 5 minutes. Unmold in shallow bowl or on lipped serving plate. Meanwhile, prepare Orange Sauce. Spoon sauce over hot baba, poking holes into the cake at ½-inch intervals to help absorb all of the sauce. If desired, garnish with almonds and maraschino cherries.

8 servings (for 3½-quart Crock-Pot). Double recipe for 5-quart Crock-Pot.

ORANGE SAUCE

½ cup frozen orange juice	½ cup sugar
concentrate, undiluted	2 tablespoons rum
½ cup water	

Combine all ingredients in saucepan. Heat to boiling, stirring to blend; remove from heat.

German Chocolate Cake

2¼ cups German chocolate
    pudding style cake mix
¾ cup water
3 tablespoons oil
2 eggs

¼ cup melted butter or
    margarine
¼ cup brown sugar
¼ cup chopped pecans
¼ cup coconut

Combine cake mix, water, oil and eggs. Beat 2 minutes.

Pour melted butter into bottom of greased and floured Bread 'n Cake Bake pan. Add brown sugar, nuts and coconut. Stir to blend well.

Pour batter over nut-coconut mixture. Place covered Bread 'n Cake Bake pan in Crock-Pot and cover. Bake on High setting 2½ to 4 hours.

12 servings For 5–quart Crock-Pot: Use 1 package (18.5 oz.) cake mix, 1¼ cups water, ⅓ cup oil and 3 eggs. Double remaining ingredients. Prepare as directed above.

A WAY WITH BREADS AND CAKES

•Do not over-beat breads and cakes. Follow recommended mixing times, usually about 2 minutes.

•Never place baking pan on meat rack.

•Do not add water to the Crock-Pot unless it is specifically requested in the recipe.

•After baking breads or cakes, allow to cool 5 minutes, then invert pan on cooling rack or plate.

Nut Pound Cake

---

1 cup butter, softened	1½ teaspoons baking
1 cup sugar	powder
3 eggs	1½ cups pecans, coarsely
1½ teaspoons vanilla	chopped
2 cups flour	

With electric mixer, cream butter, sugar, eggs and vanilla until light and fluffy. Stir flour and baking powder together; stir in pecans. Add dry ingredients to creamed mixture and mix well. Pour into greased and floured Bread 'n Cake Bake pan; cover. Place in Crock-Pot. Cover and bake on High setting for 2 to 3 hours or until cake tests done with a wooden pick.

Remove pan and uncover. Let stand 5 minutes. Unmold on cake rack.

15 servings (for 3½- or 5-quart Crock-Pot).

Applesauce Spice Cake

¼ cup butter or margarine	1 teaspoon baking soda
½ cup sugar	¼ teaspoon cinnamon
1 egg	¼ teaspoon ground cloves
½ teaspoon vanilla	¼ teaspoon nutmeg
¾ cup applesauce	½ cup raisins
1 cup flour	½ cup chopped pecans

Cream butter and sugar. Add egg and vanilla and beat well. Beat in applesauce. Combine flour, soda and spices and stir into creamed mixture. Blend in raisins and nuts.

Pour into greased and floured Bread 'n Cake Bake pan and cover. Place in Crock-Pot, cover and bake on High setting 2½ to 4 hours.

12 servings. Double recipe for 5 quart Crock-pot.

Sourdough Chocolate Cake

1 cup sugar
½ cup shortening
2 eggs
1 cup sourdough starter
    (page 184)
1 cup evaporated milk
1 teaspoon vanilla

1 teaspoon cinnamon
3 squares (1 oz. each)
    chocolate, melted
½ teaspoon salt
1½ teaspoons baking soda
2 cups flour

Cream sugar and shortening until light and fluffy. Beat in eggs, one at a time. Stir in sourdough starter, milk, vanilla, cinnamon and melted chocolate. Beat with rotary beater for 2 minutes. Blend salt and soda together until smooth. Sprinkle over batter and fold in gently. Fold in flour until batter is smooth. Pour into greased and floured Bread 'n Cake Bake pan; cover. Place in Crock-Pot. Cover and bake on High setting for 2½ to 3½ hours.

Remove pan and uncover. Let stand for 5 minutes. Unmold on cake rack and cool. Especially good when served with hot fudge sauce.

12 servings (for 3½- or 5-quart Crock-Pot).

Rich Brownies in a Nut Crust

¼ cup butter or margarine, melted
1 cup chopped nuts

1 family-size package (about 23 oz.) brownie mix

Pour melted butter into Bread 'n Cake Bake pan, swirl to butter sides. Sprinkle with half the nuts. Mix brownies according to the package directions. Pour half the batter into pan, covering nuts evenly. Add remaining half of nuts, then batter. Place Bread 'n Cake Bake pan in Crock-Pot. Cover and bake on High setting for 3 hours, or until done. Do not check or remove cover until last hour.

Let stand 5 minutes. Unmold and serve warm.

24 brownies (for 3½– or 5–quart Crock-Pot).

Layer Bars

1 package (18 oz.) chocolate chip cookie mix
½ cup chocolate chips
½ cup butterscotch chips

½ cup flaked coconut
½ cup chopped nuts
½ cup sweetened condensed milk

Prepare cookie mix according to package instructions. Place into greased Bread 'n Cake Bake pan. Layer remaining ingredients in the order listed. Do not stir. Cover pan and place in Crock-Pot. Cover and bake on High setting for 2 to 3 hours or until firm.

Remove pan and uncover. Let stand 5 minutes. Unmold carefully on plate and cool.

> *WARM-UP SESSIONS*
> •To reheat breads, cakes or puddings, wrap securely in aluminum foil and place in Crock-Pot. Cover and heat on High setting for 1 to 1½ hours (on Low setting for 2 to 3 hours).

Carrot Cake

2 eggs
1 cup sugar
⅔ cup oil
1½ cups flour
1 teaspoon baking soda
½ teaspoon salt
1 teaspoon cinnamon

¾ cup grated carrots
½ cup chopped nuts
1 can (8¼ oz.) crushed
   pineapple in syrup,
   drained
1 teaspoon vanilla

Beat together eggs, sugar and oil. Combine flour, soda, salt and cinnamon; add to sugar mixture and beat well. Stir in carrots, nuts, pineapple and vanilla.

Pour into greased and floured Bread 'n Cake Bake pan. Cover and place in Crock-Pot. Cover and bake on High setting for 2½ to 4 hours.

12 servings (3½– or 5–quart size).

Indian Pudding

3 cups milk	¼ cup sugar
½ cup cornmeal	⅓ cup molasses
½ teaspoon salt	½ teaspoon ginger
3 eggs	½ teaspoon cinnamon

Lightly grease Crock-Pot. Preheat on High setting for 20 minutes. Meanwhile bring milk, cornmeal and salt to a boil. Boil, stirring constantly, 5 minutes; cover and simmer an additional 10 minutes. In large bowl, combine remaining ingredients, then gradually beat in hot cornmeal mixture with an electric mixer or whisk until smooth. Pour into Crock-Pot. Cover and cook on High setting for 2 to 3 hours (on Low setting for 6 to 8 hours).

Spoon into serving dishes and serve warm, topped with ice cream, if desired.

6 to 8 servings (about 1½ quarts). Double recipe for 5-quart Crock-Pot.

Cottage Pudding

1¾ cups flour	¾ cup sugar
2 teaspoons baking powder	1 egg
	¾ cup milk
½ teaspoon salt	1 teaspoon vanilla
¼ cup soft shortening	

Stir together flour, baking powder and salt. Add remaining ingredients and beat until smooth. Pour into greased and floured Bread 'n Cake Bake pan; cover. Place pan in Crock-Pot. Cover and bake on High setting for 3 to 4 hours or until pudding springs back when touched lightly with finger. Do not check or remove cover until last hour of baking.

Let stand 5 minutes. Unmold and serve warm, with sweetened fresh fruit or any dessert sauce.

8 to 10 servings (for 3½– or 5–quart Crock-Pot).

NOTE: Cottage Pudding should be served right away, or it should be frozen immediately after cooling to preserve its freshness.

Jam Sponge Pudding

¼ cup cherry, strawberry or apricot jam	1½ cups flour
1 cup butter or margarine, softened	1 teaspoon baking powder
⅔ cup sugar	½ teaspoon salt
2 eggs, beaten	¼ cup water or milk

Grease Bread 'n Cake Bake pan well. Spread jam in bottom. With electric mixer, cream butter and sugar well. Add eggs gradually. Mix dry ingredients together and stir into creamed mixture with wooden spoon. Stir in water. Pour mixture over jam; cover pan. Pour ½ cup water into Crock-Pot. Place covered pan in Crock-Pot. Cover and steam on High setting for 2 to 3 hours.

Remove pan and uncover. Unmold immediately on cake rack and cool.

6 to 8 servings (for 3½- or 5-quart Crock-Pot). Use ½ cup jam for 5-quart size.

Peach Pecan Coffee Cake

1 (16 oz.) can sliced
    peaches, drained
⅓ cup brown sugar
½ teaspoon cinnamon
⅓ cup chopped pecans
1 tablespoon butter or
    margarine
2¼ cups flour

¾ cup sugar
3 teaspoons baking powder
½ teaspoon cinnamon
½ teaspoon salt
½ teaspoon nutmeg
1 cup milk
1 egg, beaten
3 tablespoons oil

Arrange peaches in bottom of greased and floured Bread 'n Cake Bake pan. Make streusel by combining brown sugar, ½ teaspoon cinnamon and chopped pecans. Sprinkle half of streusel over peaches. Dot with butter.

In a mixing bowl, stir together flour, sugar, baking powder, nutmeg, salt and remaining cinnamon. Combine milk, egg and oil; add to dry ingredients. Stir well. Pour half of batter over peaches in Bread 'n Cake Bake pan. Sprinkle with reserved streusel. Top with remaining batter. Cover Bread 'n Cake Bake pan and place in Crock-Pot. Cover and bake on High setting 2½ to 3½ hours. Invert into plate. Serve warm.

For 4 to 5 quart Crock-Pot: Use 1 (28 oz.) can sliced peaches. Increase streusel mixture to ⅔ cup brown sugar, 1 teaspoon cinnamon and ⅔ cup nuts. Dot with 2 tablespoons butter. Prepare batter and bake as directed.

Old-Fashioned Gingerbread

½ cup butter or margarine	1 teaspoon cinnamon
½ cup sugar	2 teaspoons ginger
1 egg	½ teaspoon ground cloves
1 cup light molasses	½ teaspoon salt
2½ cups flour	1 cup hot water
1½ teaspoons baking soda	

With electric mixer, cream butter and sugar. Add egg, molasses and dry ingredients; blend well. Add hot water and beat well. Pour batter into greased and floured Bread 'n Cake Bake pan and cover. Bake covered in Crock-Pot on High setting for 3 to 4 hours. Do not check or remove cover until last hour of baking.

Let stand 5 minutes. Unmold on cake rack.

8 to 10 servings (for 3½– or 5–quart Crock-Pot).

CROCK-POT BAKING TIPS

• You will note that many of these bread and cake recipes call for the use of the accessory Bread 'n Cake Bake pan. Write to Rival Manufacturing Company for ordering information.

• To achieve the best volume in your baked goods, always use large fresh eggs.

• The dough for Crock-Pot yeast breads has a different consistency than you might expect. In fact, it's more like a batter than a dough—and that's as it should be.

Cheesecake, New York Style

2 packages (8 oz. each)
  plus 1 package (3 oz.)
  cream cheese, softened
¾ cup sugar
3 tablespoons flour
1 teaspoon freshly grated
  lemon peel

½ teaspoon freshly grated
  orange peel
3 eggs
Pie Crust (below)

With electric mixer, beat softened cream cheese, sugar, flour and grated peels until smooth. Add eggs, one at a time, and beat until fluffy. Pour into baked crust in Bread 'n Cake Bake pan; cover. Set inside Crock-Pot. Cover and cook on High setting for 2½ to 3 hours.

Remove pan and uncover. Allow to cool, then unmold on serving plate. Serve well chilled; if desired, top with strawberries.

8 to 10 servings (for 3½- or 5-quart Crock-Pot).

NOTE: This cheesecake may be prepared without the crust if the pan is generously greased and floured.

PIE CRUST

⅓ cup flour
2 tablespoons sugar
½ teaspoon grated lemon
  peel

1 egg yolk
2 tablespoons butter or
  margarine, softened

In bowl, combine flour, sugar and lemon peel. Stir in egg yolk and butter. Mix with fingers until smooth. Pat out to form a crust in bottom and slightly up side of greased and floured Bread 'n Cake Bake pan. Bake in preheated 375° oven for 15 to 20 minutes.

Fruit-Nut Dessert

½ cup shortening
1 cup sugar
1 egg, lightly beaten
1½ cups flour
1 teaspoon baking soda
¾ teaspoon ground cloves

½ teaspoon cinnamon
½ cup cold coffee
½ cup chopped nuts
½ cup chopped apples
½ cup dates or raisins, chopped

With electric mixer, cream shortening and sugar. Add egg. Stir together flour, soda, cloves and cinnamon; add to creamed mixture alternately with coffee. With wooden spoon, stir in nuts and fruit. Pour into well-greased and floured Bread 'n Cake Bake pan; cover. Place in Crock-Pot. Cover and bake on High setting for 3 to 4 hours or until dessert tests done with a wooden pick.

Remove pan and uncover. Let stand 5 minutes, then unmold. Serve warm, with whipped cream.

10 to 14 servings (for 3½– or 5–quart Crock-Pot).

Rhubarb-Pineapple Compote

1 lb. fresh rhubarb
2 cups fresh pineapple chunks

½ cup orange soda
1 tablespoon sugar
Nutmeg (optional)

Wash and peel fresh rhubarb; cut into 1-inch pieces. Place fruit in Crock-Pot. Add orange soda, then sprinkle with sugar. Stir lightly. Cover and bake on High setting for about 2 hours (on Low setting for 6 to 8 hours) or until rhubarb is tender.

Serve warm or chilled. Sprinkle with nutmeg before serving.

4 to 6 servings (for 3½–quart Crock-Pot).

Nut-Filled Baked Apples

8 medium baking apples	¼ cup brown sugar
1 cup granulated sugar	(packed)
⅓ cup water	½ teaspoon cinnamon
2 tablespoons butter	1 egg
1 cup ground nuts	

Wash and core apples (do not peel). In saucepan, combine granulated sugar, water and butter; heat, stirring, until sugar is dissolved. For filling, thoroughly combine nuts, brown sugar, cinnamon and egg. Spoon filling into apples until ⅔ full. Pour syrup over the filling until cavity is filled.

Place apples on accessory Crock-Pot Rack in the Crock-Pot. Add ½ cup water. Cover and bake on Low setting for 8 to 10 hours (on High setting for 3 to 4 hours). Serve warm.

8 servings (about 3 quarts).

Apples in Wine

10 to 12 tart cooking	1 cup sugar
apples	½ teaspoon nutmeg
2 cups dry red wine	2 slices lemon (optional)

Core, peel and quarter apples. Combine wine and sugar in Crock-Pot; stir well. Add apple quarters. Stir well to coat apples with wine mixture. Add nutmeg and lemon slices. Cover and cook on Low setting for 8 to 12 hours (on High setting for 2 to 3 hours).

Transfer apples and liquid to a refrigerator container and chill well. Serve in sherbet glasses.

8 to 10 servings (about 3 quarts).

Swedish Fruit Soup

1 cup dried prunes
1 cup raisins
1 cup dried apricots
1 cup sliced apples
1 cup canned pitted red
  sour cherries
½ cup quick-cooking
  tapioca

1 cup grape juice
½ cup orange juice
¼ cup lemon juice
1 tablespoon grated orange
  peel
1 cup sugar

Combine fruits, tapioca and grape juice in Crock-Pot. Add enough water to cover (about 3 cups). Cover and cook on Low setting for 8 to 10 hours.

Before serving, gently stir in remaining ingredients. Serve warm or cold, as a soup or dessert.

10 to 12 servings (about 2½ quarts).

West Indies Apple Chutney

1 can (20 oz.) pie-sliced
  apples, drained and
  chopped
½ cup dark raisins
½ cup honey

3 tablespoons cider vinegar
¼ teaspoon salt
½ teaspoon ground ginger
½ teaspoon dry mustard
½ teaspoon curry powder

Place apples and raisins in Bread 'n Cake Bake pan. Stir together remaining ingredients. Pour over fruit and stir to blend; cover. Place pan in Crock-Pot. Cover and cook on Low setting for 6 to 8 hours (on High setting for 2 to 3 hours).

About 3 cups. Recipe may be doubled for 3½- or 5-quart Crock-Pot.

NOTE: Use smaller quantities of spices for a milder chutney.

Old-Fashioned Apple Butter

12 to 14 apples (preferably Jonathan or Winesap)	Cinnamon
2 cups apple juice	Allspice
Sugar	Cloves
	½ cup sauterne (optional)

Wash, core and quarter apples (do not peel). Combine apples and apple juice in lightly oiled Crock-Pot. Cover and cook on Low setting for 10 to 18 hours (on High setting for 2 to 4 hours).

When fruit is tender, put through a food mill to remove peel. Measure cooked fruit and return to Crock-pot. For *each pint* of sieved cooked fruit, add 1 cup sugar, 1 teaspoon cinnamon, ½ teaspoon allspice and ½ teaspoon cloves; stir well. Cover and cook on High setting for 6 to 8 hours, stirring about every 2 hours. Remove cover after 3 hours to allow fruit and juice to cook down. Add sauterne for the last hour of cooking. Spoon into hot sterilized jars and process according to standard canning methods.

About five ½-pint jars.